# Mere Motherhood

# Mere Motherhood

## MORNING TIMES, NURSERY RHYMES, AND MY JOURNEY TOWARD SANCTIFICATION

CINDY ROLLINS

CiRCE INSTITUTE

CULTIVATING WISDOM & VIRTUE

First published in the USA
by the CiRCE Institute
© Cindy Rollins 2016

ISBN: 978-0-986325-7-4-8

For information:

CiRCE Institute
81 McCachern Blvd.
Concord, NC 28025
www.circeinstitute.org

*Cover design by Graeme Pitman.*
*Layout by David Kern.*

*Printed in the United States of America.*

*To the precious and few women in my family:*

*My mother, Judy Ward, Writer and Dancer.*
*My sister, Jody Combs, Encourager and Confidante.*
*My daughter, Emily Rios, Beautiful—inside and out.*

# CONTENTS

# AUTHOR'S NOTE

*I*t is a brash thing to write a memoir, especially when it involves a family. Who really has the right to tell her side of the story? Our family story could be written eleven different ways. Some would be comedies and, sadly, some would be tragedies. Mine is a little of both. There is enough pathos to keep it from being a farce. It is easier to remember the sunny days; they offend no one. It is easy to forget the hard times; thank the Lord. So perhaps this isn't the true story of our family as much as a series of vignettes reminding us that sometimes sinners laugh and cry.

In 1984, I delivered my first son. It was like a magic trick. My doctor insisted I deliver him naturally, and naturally I complied, even though an hour in I was begging for drugs. Too late. That little boy blue was born after a labor of three hours. Nine babies later my longest labor stretched to three-and-a-half hours and my shortest a measly, awful one hour.

It appears I was made to bear babies.

We were twenty-two and twenty-three when our son was born. The biggest surprise was the hospital allowing us to take him home. How do babies survive this? I do not know, but they do, and so much more. This particular baby seemed like the baby to end all babies. He was the perfect baby, so I decided to be the perfect mother. Thirty-one years later I think he has forgiven me that hubris.

And that is how motherhood begins for most of us. We walk into a hospital and walk out with a mewling, puking wonder of the world. We went on to have nine children— eight boys and one girl. Their names are Timothy, now married to Natalia and father to five: Timtims, Blakers, Peter, David Leonidas, and Lucy; Nicholas, married to Hannah and father to Georgia, Wyatt, and Maeve; James; Nathaniel, married to Vanessa and father to Anabella and Savanna; Christopher; Benjamin; Emily, married to Anibal; Andrew; and Alex.

Some of you reading this look back on those early days of mothering through a long tunnel of memories, good times and bad. Your now fashionably gray hair is well-earned. In spite of all those surging new-mother hormones of love, you know now that motherhood is sanctification. Perhaps way more sanctification than you ever bargained for. It is not the kind of dust-bunny sanctification that makes a Facebook Meme. There is no trite way to explain the heart-wrenching joys and sorrows you have seen. There is no way to warn the mommy next door or your daughter-in-law. It is a walk of joy that often includes the tearing off of the old dragon skin one painful layer at a time, made all the worse because you didn't even know you were wearing dragon skin. No one ever does.

Some of you are new to motherhood. Your baby needs you every second of the day. You barely have time to read books. It is a time of singular joy. These days are for you to build up the good times: the nature walks and the read-alouds, the family drives and the ice cream cones. All the joy you can pack into their small lives and yours.

Perhaps the greater portion of you are in the middle years. You are just starting to panic a little bit. You are beginning to realize that tea parties don't cure sin. You want some re-assurance that all will be well when you are starting to fear it might not be. Something may go wrong. You might miss stamping out a fire or two. I think this book will be a comfort to you. You are not alone. We who have gone before are still here. We will look you in the eye and say, "Motherhood hurts like hell" but the old dragon skin does peel away. God is real. He is there. He doesn't just love your children; he loves you. I have been young, and now I am old, and I have not seen the righteous forsaken.

We do not write our own stories; we just think we do. My story belongs to Jesus, so I already know that it has a happy ending. Here are a few of the chapters.

### Nota Bene

I quote much scripture in this book. I do so intentionally, without references, because that is how I believe scripture should fit into the fabric of our lives. It is not tacked on; it is woven in.

# PROLOGUE

*I* do not think I have told more than one person this. I was visiting my parents, and they were gushing about my children as usual, but this time they were gushing about me, too. I was an excellent mother, and I had wonderful children. In the midst of my parents' encouragement, my heart swelled with pride. I thought as I drove home, "I am an excellent mother, and I have good relationships with all my children." My pride was a clear line drawn in the sand, and God, in his infinite mercy, rescued me from those sinful thoughts just like he rescued Nebuchadnezzar when he basked in the glory of his kingdom, and God caused him to eat grass like a wild beast for a season. Within a few weeks, my heart was struck and my world was shaken so violently that the only thing I could be sure of was that God was God and I was not.

I am a fixer-type, so in the first light of finding broken family relationships, I placed my confidence in my ability to make things right. I wrote letters. They made things worse. I wrote more letters somehow expecting a different result. I talked to this family member and that family member and all the while everything I touched turned to stone, especially the hearts of my children. I realized that this was a mess I could not fix and that fixer part of me died. So I was forced to let go of my children and my family and my homeschool and my lifework of thirty years, a work that had often filled me with great satisfaction. All of it was gone.

My life felt like a scene from *Mad Max*. The landscape was desolate. In that dark, terrible place I sat and waited and cried. I cried so much my eyes became inflamed and infected. But I was not alone. God was there. It felt like He was physically there and He was enough. I read my Bible, and He spoke. I read the Psalms, and He comforted. I read them again and again and again until every word seemed like it was written just for me. I was loved and held. I couldn't fix anything, but God loved me. I still cried, but I knew that God saw my tears and collected them. Sin had hurt me, and what was worse, my pride and ignorance had hurt my children, but there was a Redeemer.

One terrible day, we went to a counselor's office. We tried to communicate and tried to listen. We did both badly. When we got home, the first thing my eyes saw was Isaiah 43:18-19:

*"Remember not the former things, nor consider the things of old. Behold, I am doing a new thing; now it springs forth, do you not perceive it? I will make*

*a way in the wilderness and rivers in the desert."*

I grabbed on to that verse tightly, and I am still holding on. My life was a desert stripped of all its flora and fauna. It was a wasteland of confusion, but here I had a promise which seemed intended for me. I did not have to wallow in mourning over past sins, past mistakes, past regrets. I could let God create something new in my life as a mother, a person made in the image of God, and in my broken relationships with my children.

Since that day, I have seen these children offer forgiveness to me and others in ways that I never imagined possible. The capacity for forgiveness is beautiful, more beautiful than anything I have ever seen before. I have seen healing in broken relationships, and I have seen new relationships formed, new ways carved out of the wilderness. Streams have, indeed, begun to flow in the desert.

One of the biggest dangers homeschooling moms face is letting their relationships become idols of the heart. It is easy for this idolatry to lay dormant and festering for years and years, undiscovered, causing damage. In fact, we often misdiagnose it as righteousness. Never forget the Bible says the wages of sin is death. Christ rescued us from death, so there is no reason to substitute our Earthly relationships for our Heavenly one. Seek ye first the Kingdom of God and His righteousness and all these things will be added to you.

In the end, Christ alone is worth every sacrifice. Like Abraham, we can sacrifice our children to Christ. I like to think that all my children are 'only' children. I learned that from *Cheaper by the Dozen*.

I am less tempted to fear for my children these days. I still worry, but not as much as I used to. I know bad things will happen, but I also know that God is up to the challenge. He is trustworthy and I can give my precious family to him. I do not have to clasp them tightly in my hands. As Corrie Ten Boom said, "Hold everything in your hands lightly. Otherwise, it hurts when God pries your fingers open." He has pried my idols from my grasping fingers, but I would not return to the former days. Those days when I hid my pride even from myself, clinging to my family as if it were my Savior, loving the gift rather than the Giver.

In some ways, this is the last chapter of this book and the beginning of another story, but I tucked it in here at the start so you will remember that this is no fairytale I am writing.

# CHAPTER ONE

# Once Upon a Time

*"What matters in life is not what happens to you*
*but what you remember and how you remember it."*
**Gabriel García Márquez**

*O*nce upon a time, I was not a mother. I did not home-school. If education is an atmosphere, a discipline, and a life, as Charlotte Mason proposed, my education began the day I was born, as did yours. My interest in the subject did not trail far behind. C.S. Lewis told the story of his conversion in *Surprised By Joy*; it is the closest thing to an autobiography we have of everyone's favorite Christian thinker. Likewise, this book, while perhaps not an autobiography of my life, is a history of my education, particularly in the art of motherhood. I rather hope it is not as pompous as *The Education of Henry James*; I am a reluctant navel gazer. My friend, Dr. George Grant, says that education is repentance. If so, this is a series of repentances beginning with my childhood—a history of my sanctification.

Women have often historically been considered the more spiritually-minded sex, annoyingly so, I am afraid. Perhaps our roles as caretakers just give the Holy Spirit ample scope to humble us and remind us how little we know and how very little we control. We have to repent of that idea of control, repent of our little kingdoms over and over again. Maybe the greater part of our sanctification comes as we remember that those around us were not born as appendages to us; they are unique individuals made in the image of God. In return, we are not appendages to our family either. I was born a person. My mother found this just as shocking about me as I did about my first son.

Recently, a friend was getting ready to study a book on mothering for a reading group. One of the mothers in the group balked. She could not bear to read another book about an idyllic family. It hurt too much. Even as I write, today is Mother's Day. Outwardly, I am feigning indifference. I know my children love me, even when they don't always like me, nor I them. What does it matter if they send me a card or flowers or presents? But inwardly, I am counting off the remembrances with some fear.

It is a despicable holiday in many ways. On the surface it is a wonderful idea. Let's all appreciate our mothers! What could possibly be wrong with that? And yet, woman after woman anguishes over the day. Children are given the impossible task of appreciating their mothers. We all know it is hooey, but we can't just ignore it, either. We can't let our mothers down. What mother/child relationship could not be dubbed, "it's complicated?" Maybe as mothers we even have a little sense of entitlement. Once we have given over our bodies to another human being for nine months it's hard to step back and not demand some sort of repayment. The words trip out so easily, "After all I have done for you. . . ." The real story is that when we seek validation from any source other than Christ we are going to be disappointed. Mother's Day is disappointing, and books about happy families are disappointing, and our own hearts are disappointing.

In a sermon called "The Word of Jesus on Prayer," George MacDonald reminds us that "everything difficult indicates something more than our theory of life suggests." Motherhood is a place of dreamy hopes and crushed fantasies and the hard, hard work of sinners in relationship with one another day by day. But sometimes all nine children call and text and send us beautiful cards and gifts and say they love us in chorus. What a beautiful harmony that is.

This interest in education, this history of repentance, this trajectory of sanctification is my story. Was it nature or nurture, my interest in eduction? You will not find the answer here. My father was a coach and a teacher. My mother taught dancing and Head Start. Every single one of my aunts and uncles were teachers, and now all of my cousins and my sister are, as well. We lived on college campuses throughout my childhood. My parents read books in their spare time, and I often read what they were reading, age appropriate or not. My mother was not a fan of rewarding children for good grades, so she overcompensated by rarely even glancing at my report card. This used to bother me, but now I see it kept me from getting caught up in the system. Learning was never irrevocably tied to school in my mind by grades. My dad often waxed eloquent about the liberal arts. I suppose he had fined-tuned his thoughts while recruiting baseball players.

The day I was born my father was at a baseball game. Eventually, this would make some sense out of my life, but that day it just made my mother mad. I was born in Cincinnati, home of the Big Red Machine and Skyline Chili. As a young girl, there were no signs that I would someday go crazy and have nine children. My mother was straight out of *Mad Men* with her chiffon dresses and high-heeled pumps. I would take all of her lovely heels out of the closet and play shoe store for hours. Sometimes, in between the soap operas, we would cuddle up on the couch and read nursery rhymes.

When I was two, my brother Scott joined us. When I was four, we moved to Fort Pierce, Florida, where my Dad coached baseball at Indian River Community College. Our house, with a terrarium in the living room and Palazzo floors, was across the street from the beach. Mom, Scott, and I walked to the beach daily, turning our hair into white cotton. When I was six, my sister and my friend, Jody, was born. We had moved on campus by that time so my dad could walk to work, but we couldn't walk to the beach anymore.

My life was probably negatively shaped, or maybe providentially shaped (who knows how these things work) by starting school at a younger age than most. I began regular kindergarten at four. I started first grade at five. I went to college at sixteen and I married at eighteen. My entire school career I cowered in the back of the classroom, hoping no one would notice me. Hardly anyone did. For twelve years I was tormented by my schooling. Dazed by my surroundings, I learned little.

I cried in first grade when Mrs. Jesse called on me to sound out the word B-A-T. I also cried when she paddled my five-year-old hand with a ruler for some unknown misdemeanor. I cried again when she gave us an 8x10 glossy of her son-in-law Lurch. Yes, that Lurch. Waking up in the middle of the night to a picture of Lurch leering at you is scary.

By the time I was in second grade, we lived in DeLand, Florida, where my dad took a job as baseball coach to the Stetson University Hatters. My brother and I started hanging out with dad on campus to get us "out of Mom's hair." We sat under the live oaks, putting trumpet vines on our fingers, absorbing the college scene. We spent our first Greek Week under a bush watching the fun (or, at least, some of it). I spent many days puzzling over words like "gymnasium." The liberal arts had already captured my imagination.

When I was seven Scott and I started walking to Boston Avenue Elementary School every morning. He was five. We would stop by a tiny old house on the way and pick up our friends the Pinkneys. Their dad was the iconic shoeshine man in DeLand and a bit of a celebrity. As a testament to how thoroughly times have changed in the last fifty years, I am shocked now when I drive from our old home on S. Amelia Avenue to Boston Avenue; it was a long walk. I cannot imagine letting such small children walk it, but I have only happy and vivid memories of those walks to school. How much learning did I process along the way?

My second grade class was in the dark basement auditorium of Boston Avenue. Our family was attending church now at the Christian and Missionary Alliance, located on the campus of a retired missionary's home. I had heard exciting stories straight out of Africa about God's provision, and so I told my teacher I wanted to be a missionary when I grew up. This was the best way to be in God's will, I had learned.

In third grade I fell in love with a brave sea captain in a

reader; I have never been able to find him again, although I have scoured book sales. I also learned never to start a sentence with "because." Because it is just not done. The sea captain captured my imagination; grammar did not.

In DeLand, eighth and ninth grades were housed in a charming ancient building surrounded by live oaks, called The Junior High. In eighth grade, sex-ed did not capture my imagination, thank goodness. We watched *Gone with the Wind* at the Athens Theater in downtown DeLand, Florida, and I went on to read the book over and over and over again, each time hoping Rhett would give a damn. In ninth grade, my English teacher read my poems and started encouraging me to write more. We had an eight-week session on grammar, none of which I remember. But I do remember Jonathan Livingston Seagull, Romeo and Juliet, and a teacher who cared about an invisible girl with a notebook full of poems.

In our family, spring was baseball season. From the time February rolled around until late May, most afternoons were spent at Conrad Park watching Stetson play baseball. When I was still little, I played dolls in the cavernous spaces under the bleachers. When I was around twelve, I chased the toddler Chipper Jones (later to become the iconic Atlanta Braves baseball player) around while his dad played baseball for my dad. When I was sixteen, I sat in the bleachers trying to look pretty. To this day when February rolls around, I am ready for baseball, and I proudly say, "My dad is Jim Ward." For over fifty years baseball has been my constant.

In eleventh grade, I did something odd in my quest to disappear. The Daytona Beach Community College was offering a new program in which you could attend classes for a couple of months and graduate early from high school. My best friend, Sandra, and I did just that. I asked my dad to sign the paper, and he did, later claiming he had no idea what I was talking about. I took a few classes at the community college and graduated from high school. My high school principal said I would regret it because the community college was not an accredited high school, but just after that, DeLand High School lost its accreditation temporarily due to drug issues. This was the 1970s in Florida, but I was paying attention; accreditation was not all that.

I was sixteen and out of high school. I still had only learned what I had serendipitously picked up in books. I had voraciously plowed through the DeLand Public Library, but I was not yet awake.

After graduating, I was not sure what to do, so my parents sent me to live with my grandmother in Cincinnati for a few months. I worked in a calendar factory. Some co-workers had been there for over thirty years. It was interminably dull. Their only solace seemed to be their smoke breaks. With so much smoke around I shocked my grandmother by buying a pack of cigarettes. One night, I sat outside on the front stoop looking at the stars and the outlines of the trees and smoking, just like my deceased and well-loved grandfather had done before he died of a heart attack. I didn't feel glamorous at all. I felt like a fifty-year-old factory worker, and so that was the end of that. I wanted to go home and to college. I did not want to be a factory worker looking forward to my next smoke break.

I decided to take a couple of classes at Stetson University where Dad still coached. I took Psychology and freshman

English. My English professor loved my papers. He would read them out loud while I beamed with joy. My poor dad suffered through my semester in psychology as I constantly enlightened him on how to coach via Pavlov. Thankfully, none of my own children have been quite that obnoxious.

I was starting to like college. People invited me to parties. I was thinking of not being invisible anymore. Then my dad did something terrible: he accepted a coaching position at Eastern Kentucky University. My scholarship to Stetson was gone. I gave my dad a piece of my mind which, I guess, now that I am a mother, made him feel horrible and guilty. But I went to Lake Swan Camp that summer and talked to a girl from Toccoa Falls Bible College. She encouraged me to join her there, and since I had already visited the campus with our youth group from church several times, I told my parents I wanted to go to Toccoa. They were relieved, I think, that I was not going to be moping around our new home in Kentucky giving them pieces of my mind on a regular basis.

I struggled through my first semester at Toccoa. In spite of not being an Ivy League of the South University like Stetson, my English teacher, Miss Roberta Swagger, was much stricter than my professor at Stetson. She did not gush about my papers. For the first time in my life, I had to work hard in class. And then it happened.

Toccoa had what was called a Winterim semester lasting two weeks. That year, Professor James Patterson helped get the film series *How Shall We Then Live* by Francis Schaeffer into the class. I gave my whole attention to that series, with its sweeping view of western civilization from a Christian perspective. Somehow, some way, during that week I woke up. Francis Schaeffer captured my imagination with ideas. I became aware that I had missed something important along the way. I knew nothing, I realized, and I needed to fix that. By the time the medieval congregation on the screen was singing "A Mighty Fortress" in the cathedral, I was sobbing in my pew in the little chapel of Toccoa Falls College. My baptized imagination was awakening to truth, beauty, and goodness, and I was going to spend the rest of my life trying to catch up. I was eighteen.

§

I was seventeen when I initially arrived on the campus of Toccoa Falls College, nestled in the foothills of North Georgia, and famous for its 186-foot waterfall. A vast forest of green and mist, Toccoa was as unlike Florida as a place could be.

I had visited the campus three or four times in high school with my church youth group. Our annual trip to the campus was the highlight of the church year for me.

On my first visit, in ninth grade, an older college girl housed my best friend, Sandra, and me in her dorm room. For some reason, she shared with us the then-popular notion that God had revealed to her whom she was going to marry. She never did marry the fellow, but to me and Sandra this was fodder for the silly mill. After all, we were in all the throes of giggling girlhood.

One afternoon Sandra and I hiked to the top of the falls, and as we were climbing we ran across a couple of high school guys who were also climbing. We spoke to them momentarily and learned that one was Tim Rollins from Lake Swan Camp, our church camp. He was the younger brother of all those handsome Rollins waterskiing instructors. A younger Rollins! After we had said our goodbyes, we immediately started back to giggling, Sandra saying, "I think it is God's will that you marry Tim." We kept laughing, but I also added a bit of pondering in my heart.

My mother later told me that when she dropped me off at college that first semester I kept saying, "There's Tim Rollins, but I don't like him." She didn't believe me. I believed me because I was already in a long-distance relationship with a baseball player from Yale. How could I like Tim? And, besides, Tim had a few fish on his line, too.

Tim was originally from Savannah, Georgia, with a beautiful drawl to prove it. His father was what was then called a pioneer pastor, planting Christian and Missionary Alliance churches all over the south. Tim was as southern and as gentlemanly as a person could be. As freshmen, we were often thrown together. He even asked me to go hiking a few times. I loved hiking, so I went along, and Tim was tall, dark, and handsome. He also liked to read the Bible with me, and that was a powerful draw. I was earnest that first semester of Bible college. I had given up pina coladas and rock music, throwing away both my albums and my dad's in a fit of conscience. It is hard to believe my dad still speaks to me.

Tim and I didn't think of ourselves as dating until the Sadie Hawkins Hay Ride. I always had a mortal fear of Sadie Hawkins events. I do not know if it was a late 1970s thing, or a Christian youth group thing, but I had more than enough of Sadie Hawkins. My usual mode was to pick someone I did not know or ignore the event altogether. I did not ask Tim to the Sadie Hawkins Hay Ride until he finally hinted around that I should. That should have alerted him that I was more than a little high-minded. Finally, on a hike, I asked him if he would be my date and he said yes, but he was a little bitter it had taken me so long. The hay ride started on campus and wound through the mountain trails until it arrived at an old tobacco barn where a band played bluegrass music. As the temperature dropped and we cuddled up to stay warm, the hay wagon took us back to campus. That romantic ride sealed our fate. We were a couple.

In truth, the guy from Yale was the nicest guy I had ever known, but I wanted a 'spiritual' man. Being seventeen meant I did not have the slightest clue what that word 'spiritual' meant, but it was the cry of my heart. Tim was the most spiritual guy I had met on campus, with his invitations to prayer and Bible study. One day as I was looking all over campus for him, I ran into his roommate, Danny, who was looking for him, too. Danny said, "Maybe the Lord came again and decided only to take Tim." That was the guy I wanted, the guy the Lord wanted. Even an amateur psychologist can see this was an awful lot of pressure to place on a man and a marriage.

Sadie Hawkins was in October. In March, we traveled from Toccoa to Richmond, Kentucky, to meet my parents during spring break. My mother thought we were there to ask my father's permission to get married, so during one of those awkward family dinners with the boyfriend, she made it even more awkward by asking (in front of everyone) if Tim wanted to ask my dad something. He did not. But not long afterward, in April, we walked to the falls only to find it busy with tourists. Tim then said, "Let's go over to the little falls." This was a hidden treasure on campus, tucked behind an old electric company building. His mother had given him her beautiful antique engagement ring, which took me by surprise since I knew he couldn't afford a ring. There, behind the little falls, he knelt on one knee and asked me to marry him. I was not entirely surprised, of course; I had been hoping. I was eighteen, and he was nineteen. He was the youngest of six children, and all of his siblings were married. I was a girl who thought "I love you," should be followed by "Will you marry me?" For some reason, no one tried to stop us. No one said, "You are too young." Maybe we were, maybe we weren't. We thought we would get married in two years, but after we got engaged every conversation pushed the date forward. By the end of the semester, the date was set for July 26, 1980, just two months away.

That summer we both worked at Lake Swan Camp in Melrose, Florida, making almost no money. Lake Swan was a couple of hours from my hometown of DeLand, and although my parents didn't live there anymore, that was where we wanted to get married. It was a stressful time. On our day off each week, we traveled to DeLand to take care of all the details. In the evenings at camp, we filled out wedding invitations. We were married in the DeLand Alliance Church. Our wedding was simple but pretty enough not to look too dated in pictures. Tim's dad officiated. We laugh now because this was Florida in July, and the church air conditioning broke. As we knelt to pray, sweat poured down our faces. Today, even without the heat, we often fast forward through his father's long prayer when listening to the cassette tape of our wedding. It was an exceedingly long prayer. Tim, who has a lovely voice, sang, "Let Me See This World Through Your Eyes, O, Lord" at our wedding, and that song was our prayer. We thought we would go to the mission field someday.

We returned to camp after our honeymoon on the beach. Would you believe there was a Sadie Hawkins at camp that first week back? Only, this Sadie Hawkins required the girl to chase her date and tag him. I was not going to participate, but some girl who hadn't heard that Tim was married started chasing him, so I humbled myself once more and caught him. You could call that our first fight.

After camp ended, we headed back to Toccoa. That first year of marriage we lived off campus in a little cabin in the woods. It was idyllic. Tim worked at Sherriff's Best Buy, a grocery store, and I worked at Happy Corner, a day care center. All the while, we were still attending college. By some fluke, Tim decided to take an upper-level class taught by Dr. Kay Ludwigson called "Oxford Christians." He came home excited about the class and introduced me to the authors he heard about for the first time—C.S. Lewis, J.R.R. Tolkien, Dorothy Sayers, and Charles Williams. Coming on the heels of my earlier awakening during *How Shall We Then Live*, I plunged into their imaginative worlds. I read constantly, and when I got to *The Last Battle* in *The Chronicles of Narnia*, I called in sick to work; it was the appropriate thing to do. *The Last Battle* captured not only my imagination but my Christian imagination. For the first time in my life, I caught a glimpse of Heaven as an appealing place.

During this time of mental sowing, we babysat our nephew Michael, who was three, while his parents went on a mission trip. I had such a lovely time with Michael. I took him to the bookstore and bought him a couple of little paperback children's books. When my sister-in-law, Gina, heard how excited I was to be reading to Michael, she suggested a book called *Honey for a Child's Heart* by Gladys Hunt. I ordered it immediately even though at the time we were scrounging through pockets for change to buy gas. *Honey for a Child's Heart* is about reading to children, and it had a list of the best children's books to read, which I poured over again and again for years. It quickly became one of my greatest resources.

Tim and I did not have any children yet, but *Honey for a Child's Heart* started to shape how we wanted to raise them when we did. In the meantime, we got a dog named Wimpy, a golden retriever/beagle mix. If only I could have read to him. I am not quite sure I didn't.

The ideas flowing into my life were coming furiously, tripping over each other.

Every day at around 11:00 A.M., I would tune into a new 15-minute radio show called Focus on the Family with host Dr. James Dobson, a psychologist, and a Christian. One day, Dr. Dobson interviewed a man named Raymond Moore who spoke of a form of education I'd never heard of: homeschooling. When Tim came home for lunch that day I told him that I knew what we were going to do with our imaginary children. We were going to homeschool them. Tim was not amused, but since we didn't actually have any children, he let it go. I, of course, bought another book, *Better Late than Early* by Drs. Raymond and Dorothy Moore.

I worked at a daycare center at a time when preschool was

considered the best thing you could do for your child. While Phil Donahue, my hero, touted preschool as the most beneficial thing for young children, I was sitting on the playground trying to give parental love to forty children. By the time we put Scooby Doo on every afternoon at 4:00 I was exhausted and frustrated. I could not replace these children's parents, and it didn't take that long every day to teach them a few letters and numbers. When the mothers came to pick the children up they (both parents and children) were exhausted and frustrated, too. I wondered how a parent could afford to put a child in daycare. Shouldn't daycare be worth more than working at the factory? Shouldn't the people caring for the children be valued more highly? To this day, I don't understand this economy. The people watching and teaching our children should be the ones making the money. Our schools should not be suffering from lack of funds. Our children get a vivid picture every day in their schools of the value society places on them.

Things went well in Toccoa until Tim lost his job. He left the grocery store to work construction, but when the recession of the 1980s hit, he was laid off. We picked up everything to move to North Carolina where Tim's brother-in-law Bill worked in nuclear power. Tim started working alongside him and still works in that field today. I started waitressing on the beach, a job I only held for a few months. I missed college terribly, and our dream of being missionaries took another direction entirely.

At this point, we started to think about children. I had already had one miscarriage which had left me emotionally vulnerable. Now I had another one. These miscarriages took me completely by surprise. When I had the first one I didn't even know what a miscarriage was. I woke up one morning cramping and sick. I hadn't even realized I was pregnant. When I went to the doctor he called it an abortion which confused me. I was only nineteen and when I told people I was having a miscarriage they mostly said, "Oh, you must be so relieved." This puzzled me. Maybe I was relieved. For six months, I suppressed any mourning over the loss, telling everyone flippantly it was a good thing I wasn't pregnant, until finally my body and spirit rebelled against such a cavalier attitude. After six months, I broke down and mourned bitterly for that little lost life. By the time I miscarried a second time, I had learned enough to grieve immediately, but mourning is exhausting, and I wondered how much of it I could take. Could I bear to have more miscarriages? After four years of marriage, we still had no children. Would we be childless?

Tim was only a contractor, which meant that he worked outages at power plants but did not have a permanent position. Sometimes he was out of work. During one emotional jobless stint, I told him that I could work, or I could have children, but I couldn't do both. This took him by surprise. His mother had worked off-and-on during his teen years, but he had always sensed her guilt about it. I could not see the point of having children only to put them in daycare. In what we now consider a providential turning in our lives, Tim said, "Give your two weeks' notice." I did, and by the end of those two weeks I was throwing up, and Tim had a job that paid twice as much as the previous one.

We were going to be a family.

# CHAPTER TWO

# Wynken, Blynken & Nod

*"The most extraordinary thing in the world is an ordinary man and an ordinary woman and their ordinary children."*
**G.K. Chesterton**

The miscarriages had left me with a deep fear that I would never bear a live child, but then there we were: Tim, my mother, Dr. Pole, and me, trying to have a natural birth. Dr. Pole was a unique doctor in those days. He firmly believed in natural child birth. We didn't have to convince him of our birth plan; he was pushing his on us. A few minutes after he broke my water I was in pain, and shortly thereafter I was refused an epidural. Then, after I pushed for one very long hour, there was Timothy. I was a mother—sheer joy distilled in my heart for the rest of my life. The first twenty-four hours of a baby's life are magic. I have enjoyed those hours nine times. That is a lot of joy for one life.

We dressed him up in a tiny white smocked outfit still too big for him and took him home. Why had they allowed us to take him home? We knew nothing at all about this fragile creature.

Tim's job required that we follow the power outages of nuclear plants, staying a few weeks to a few months in each new town, so we traded our tiny Nissan for a station wagon and hit the road with our baby. Every town we lived in I put Timothy in a front pack and walked all over the place, but mostly to the libraries. In South Carolina, where we moved first, we began reading aloud in earnest. By the time Timothy was six weeks old we were reading Winnie-the-Pooh poems and nursery rhymes. A doctor's wife told me I had better put him in a crib in his own room and get him out of my bed, so I put him in the room down the hall, and then I mourned. I missed him. We had each other, Tim and me, but he, our baby, was down the hall all by himself. I could not do it. Back he came. Now I didn't have to worry about him all night long. He was there with me and he was safe.

When he was six weeks old, I found a library book called *Teach Your Baby to Read* by Glen Doman. I had been reading about homeschooling for four years and was itching to take it out on someone. Tim was itching for me to find a different pupil beside himself. I loved spending time with Timothy so much that sometimes I would wake him up from his nap just to read and play. After twenty years of sleeplessness, this now seems insane, but I was having so much fun. I started holding up flashcards in front of him Glen Doman-style. I did this for a few weeks before I realized how silly I was. Timothy took it all in stride.

Even though I was having fun being a mother and traveling around, I was terrified of the mice in our trailer in South

Carolina. Another nuclear contractor from New York City stayed with us one night. He explained how mice ate babies' toes in the middle of the night in Brooklyn, fueling my fears that the trailer was a bad place for a baby. I planted mouse traps all over the trailer, including in front of the stove where on more than one occasion I stepped on it with bare feet. Pavlov was right: for years, I cooked standing several feet away from the stove, bending over awkwardly. It was a relief when years later I realized no trap would snap my toes if I stepped in closer to the stove. Some people might have opted for shoes.

One snowy January day when Timothy was six-months-old we moved to Peru, Nebraska, a little town on the prairie. Tim dropped us off at our new home, then headed off to work. I unpacked our few belongings and began to set up the house. I needed to get the water and electricity turned on but there was no phone line, so I hiked half a mile to town, with Timothy bundled in a backpack, to use a pay phone. No one answered the phone at the electric company or the phone company or the water company. Everyone was out for lunch. So we trudged back home through the snow.

A few minutes later we got a visitor.

"Heard you moved in," said an older man in workman's overalls. "Thought you might need electricity."

He was the electric company's man and he had heard through the active Peru grapevine that we were moving in. Within minutes, the phone guy showed up too, and then the water man. Not too many people were moving to Peru, Nebraska, in the middle of a snow storm. Nebraska is not the south, but it might as well have been with its friendly, easy ways.

Timothy and I explored the whole town, which looked like a stand-in for an old western movie set. The storefronts were all facades bigger than the actual store behind them. We walked to the library and the doughnut shop. We read, played, and fished on the Missouri River, and Timothy anxiously waited at the window for Papa to come home. Tim and I had so many things we wanted to share with him.

But then it was time to move on again. We headed to Rockford, Illinois, where we got to know many friends at a new church. Having grown up in the small denomination of The Christian and Missionary Alliance, we found it easy to plug ourselves into local churches wherever we moved. Timothy and I watched Tim, now called Papa, play football on crisp autumn Saturdays with the men from church. And when it got colder, Timothy would watch the snow fall through his bedroom window.

My neighbor had a baby, too, but he drove her crazy so she offered to babysit Timothy if I would watch her son several times a week. But I didn't want a break. I was loving every minute I had with Timothy.

And then one day I felt queasy.

How could I love another baby when my heart was so full with the first? It could not be possible to love like that again, but it was. My heart expanded. So much love, I thought my heart would break. Of course, it did.

Right before this new baby was born, we left Illinois where snow still covered the ground, and took off for Arizona where it was getting on towards one hundred degrees. We would only be there a few weeks, just enough time to have

our baby. We decided to have "it" at home. Home was a fur-
nished apartment. We found a midwife—no begging for an
epidural at home. We named this second son Nicholas because I loved the little boy Nicholas on the old TV show *Eight
is Enough,* and because my birthday was on St. Nicholas' Day.
Two little boys. Time for the Land's End matching outfits. As
I basked in the glow of my baby, I heard a workman outside
our apartment window say, "Did you hear she had a baby
inside that apartment?"

"No way!" said his co-worker.

I felt like a brave pioneer woman.

Nicholas loved me that first year, and just me. For one year
I could not move two steps from him, which was fine, as far
as I was concerned. Then he loved his brother too.

South Carolina, Georgia, Massachusetts. We continued to
cross the country as Tim followed the outages.

A week or two before Thanksgiving, Tim took a job near
Plymouth, Massachusetts. He traveled ahead of us to find a
home and at Thanksgiving I excitedly met him there. Boston
and Plymouth were home to much of the history I had read
about, and I was deeply affected at the opportunity to feast in
Plymouth, where the first Thanksgiving took place. I felt like
a pilgrim. We visited Boston and made way for ducklings and
spent a day at Plimoth Plantation. The history and literature I
had been discovering were coming alive.

At Easter, our Greek neighbors colored one egg deep red
to symbolize the blood of Jesus and a new Rollins family tradition was born. In fact, the traditions began to pile up. We
put cranberries and popcorn on our Christmas tree, we sang
Michael Card's "The Lord Bless You and Keep You" before

bedtime, and we had egg casserole at holiday breakfasts. Tradition was addicting.

Now I used a stroller and a backpack for our walks to the library, which was right down the road from our house on Cape Cod. We met lots of golden retrievers but hardly any other children.

§

No one I met in Massachusetts had ever heard of homeschooling. When I mentioned it at church, everyone thought I was crazy, and this made me feel like it might be a bad idea after all.

One night, Tim and I had to go to a work Christmas party, so we left the boys with some friends and on the way there we discussed how discouraged I was about the idea of homeschooling. I didn't know anyone who was doing it. It was probably a ridiculous idea.

We sat down at the circular party table, surrounded by the raucous contractor crowd, feeling the heavy burden of discouragement. I turned to the lady next to me and said, "Where do your children go to school?" She smiled and said, "We homeschool." Her name was Sharon Pangelinan. It turned out Sharon and her husband Ed not only homeschooled their two children; they had even gone to jail for homeschooling in Alabama where it was illegal to do so without a teaching certificate, but they had homeschooled in spite of the law. I grabbed onto her and did not let go until we left Massachusetts.

A few weeks later they took us to our first curriculum fair

and introduced us to the famous author of Alpha-Phonics, Sam Blumenfeld. We were among homeschool royalty. Up until then we thought of homeschooling as something we would do for just a few elementary years, perhaps through third grade. After that weekend at the curriculum fair both Tim and I were committed for the long haul. Tim had forgotten that he had ever thought it was a bad idea.

The only thing left for us to do now was buy more books.

Nicholas was growing, and since we had left all of our big stuff in storage back in Georgia, we needed a high chair. I couldn't keep chasing him around while he rode his scooter, trying to stuff food in his mouth. So Tim budgeted some money for me to buy a high chair and off I went straight to the bookstore. And that's when I discovered a book that would change my life.

There on the remainder table at the Christian bookstore was Susan Schaeffer Macaulay's *For the Children's Sake*. Of course, the title and the pretty cover grabbed my attention, but when I read on the back that the author was the daughter of Francis Schaeffer, the guy from *How Shall We Then Live*, the guy who gave me the idea to think a thought, I had to buy that book. Then I bought one or two more books because now we owned a bookcase and it had to be filled. I went to Goodwill to purchase the high chair. I bought a ratty old high chair and a few more books, including a book called *Breastfeeding and Natural Child Spacing*. We had decided to 'trust God' for our family size, and that book seemed like a good idea.

Tim took all this book-buying in stride. He had learned about my math skills when we lived in Nebraska when he had given me money to buy a dress for a friend's wedding, and I purchased a vintage prairie dress from an antique store which I could barely squeeze into owing to the fact that people were tinier in the olden days. I borrowed a dress for the wedding and carried that prairie dress around for years, hanging it on the walls rather than my body until dry rot set in.

But here in Massachusetts, I had just hit the motherlode of ideas. I went home, put the boys down for their nap, and read. *For the Children's Sake* told the story of the Macaulays stumbling upon the ideas of an English educator named Charlotte Mason. Mason, who lived from 1842-1923, was a close observer of children and came to believe that children were "born persons" who required proper food for their minds in the same way they needed bodily nourishment. She taught young teachers that children were capable of understanding real ideas, not just drivel predigested for them. The young Macauley girls were enjoying Shakespeare and Plutarch, becoming intimate with beautiful artwork, and listening with interest to the best music. The Charlotte Mason ideas Susan Macauley described in this book took hold of my mind and heart. I longed for this "living" education, based on real books and real music and real art, for my children. I longed for it for myself. My own education had been sporadic and dismal. Could it be reclaimed?

In those early days, homeschooling was a new idea. The vast majority of new homeschoolers came from listening to those 1980s Focus on the Family broadcasts. Many Christian parents were fleeing the public schools out of fear. Their sinful pasts made them fear for their children. I had been too shy to sin much in high school; at least, I didn't sin overtly in a way that left scars and regrets. What I regretted was my education. I had made straight A's in school but understood that I knew nothing. I resented the deep gaps in my education. Knowing how dismal my own education had been, I was pretty sure I could do better with my children. It would have been hard to do worse. I didn't start homeschooling out of fear, and I am happy about that now, because fear does damage wherever it appears. Later, I would fill my mind with fearful thoughts about the culture. I would listen to fear mongers and gurus. I would make bad decisions about parenting and homeschooling because of fear, but I can truthfully say that my original plan for homeschooling came entirely from a sense of excitement and joy, knowing I could give my children what I had missed.

After reading *For the Children's Sake*, I went on a quest to find Charlotte Mason's original writings. That was going to take a while. In the meantime, the only materials available to homeschoolers were Abeka and Bob Jones, Christian school publishers who had a mortal fear someone would cheat on a test by using a teacher's manual. It would not take too long for these publishers to realize there was a market ripe for harvest.

I had still not bought any curriculum because I was too busy reading Beatrix Potter and Robert McCloskey to the boys.

Then it happened again: the nausea hit right as we found out it was time to move again, this time to Millersville, Pennsylvania.

I had always thought of Pennsylvania as steel mills and

big cities with bad baseball teams, but I quickly saw that I had been wrong. Pennsylvania was lovely, with its woods and rolling hills.

On arrival, we booked ourselves into a farm bed-and-breakfast. The boys, four and two now, excitedly followed the farmer around as he showed them the inner workings of the farm. And I played Scrabble with the farmer's wife in the evenings. On the weekends, the B&B was full, so we had to check into a nearby motel. One weekend, I drove Tim thirty miles to work, took the car, and booked us into the Red Roof Inn. Then the boys and I went to look at houses. The last one we looked at was a townhouse in the country across from a Mennonite farm. While I was talking to the landlord, the boys crawled all over the station wagon, and because they were probably thirsty or maybe just plain ornery, they drank some brake fluid. I opened the back of the wagon to see them sipping the bottle.

I was in a terrible position. Tim was thirty minutes away, and he didn't know where we were. The boys might have only tasted the brake fluid; after all, it had to have tasted horrible. Surely they wouldn't have gulped it down? I decided to drive the thirty miles to pick Tim up since I could figure out no other way to alert him to our whereabouts. I spent the entire trip crying, lecturing, and questioning the boys. I prayed they lived until we got back to town. They lived, but I would need to keep ipecac on hand. We rented the brake fluid house in the end, and we spent a happy couple of years there. We only needed the ipecac once, when Nicholas ate some berries outside. I asked my lovely Mennonite neighbor if they were poisonous. "Why, yes," she calmly replied. I not so calmly ran for the syrup.

One memorable night, the little boys hollered for us because they had seen something in our garbage bag out back. Tim immediately grabbed a bat and headed outside. He came close to hitting the garbage bag when he decided discretion was the better part of valor. He stepped back as a skunk waddled out of the bag. Tim made for the house immediately. When he came in, he asked Timothy, "What do you do if you see a skunk?" Timothy replied, "Grab a bat." He was never one to run.

My last baby had been two weeks late, and now this baby was overdue. My sister Jody was visiting to help us out, but soon she would have to go home. So I decided to try an old Amish remedy, castor oil, to encourage my body to go into labor. As you can see, I am not a patient person. The castor oil tasted like liquid Vaseline, which is why this was the only time I ever tried it, and while it did make me cramp, my labor still did not begin. My new midwife, Pat, dropped by to check on me and said, "No baby today," and left. So Jody, Tim, and I pulled out the Monopoly board. We played for about thirty minutes when suddenly my water broke. Pat rushed back. Within an hour I felt the urge to push but she just laughed, saying it was wishful thinking. But only moments later she yelled, "Dammit!" as the baby boy came rushing out in the shower. "Always trust the mother."

This was James: the easiest baby ever. He sat in his swing watching his brothers shoot each other with pieces of toast they had chewed to the shape of guns. When I let him out of the swing, he grabbed the legs of anyone walking by and held on tightly, allowing them to drag him wherever they were going. It was hard to avoid his hitchhiking, whether you were a friend or stranger. He had places to go. He still does.

Our lives were starting to take on a routine. Timothy was in Awana, so I worked with him on his Bible verse every morning, and we started reading aloud from longer and longer books. He was only four, but he would listen for hours and then spend time acting out stories with Nicholas. He especially liked to act out nursery rhymes, and we had quite a repertoire of skits based on them. As he neared five, he grew increasingly logical, which drove his brother Nicholas, who was not quite three, crazy. Nicholas could never get the upper hand in any argument until one day he hit upon the perfect line. Every time Timothy tried to tell him what to do Nicholas would retort, "Papa said," and Timothy would immediately back down. This worked until one day he tried it on me when he wanted a cookie. Timothy immediately discerned if it didn't work with me, it needn't work with him either.

While the boys did fight occasionally, they were also wonderfully close. Often when we cuddled on the couch to read, they were holding hands.

Then I felt it again, my old friend nausea. This time, I embraced it, because a few months before I had been pregnant with a simpler pregnancy: no nausea, no fatigue, and, in the end, no baby.

I have never been one of those women who love pregnancy. I always found it strange that women who only have one child often talk about how much they loved being pregnant. I did not love my first pregnancy, and I did not love any of the others. How can a woman like it when her body is hijacked for nine months by a force which first makes you sick as a dog, then causes you to randomly fall asleep? And when you finally feel better you are so big you can barely hobble around and your main concern is the location of the nearest bathroom? Yes, of course, it is exciting to feel the baby move, but much of the time that is not even the baby. No, I am not one of *those* women.

After my fourth baby, it dawned on me that labor was always going to be horrific. To this day, I remember the sinking feeling that came over me when I found out I was pregnant again. I once read a comical story about a dad who was always starting projects without an end game. He finally ended up building a boat in the basement of his home before realizing there was no way to get it out. That was how I felt when I found out I was pregnant again. Getting this boat out of the basement was going to hurt. I started having panic attacks about labor. I would lie in bed and stare at the baby pictures and imagine their births and my heart would race, and I would break out in a sweat. This would happen for weeks on end. But what got me through was the babies. I loved the babies. I loved the eye contact and the nursing and the cuddling. If only I didn't have to go through labor.

And then it was time to move yet again. It seemed to be a pattern: I got nauseated, we moved. But this time it was to a permanent job. It was a little rough dragging three children around the country in a station wagon that couldn't carry all of our possessions. So we said goodbye to Mrs. Hostetter, my Mennonite friend, and our daily tea parties, and set off to New Jersey. We were going to live in Yankee Country for the next thirteen years.

# CHAPTER THREE

# Now We Are Six

*"Anybody who has survived his childhood has enough
information about life to last him the rest of his days."*
**Flannery O'Connor**

W e rented a dark little house in Vineland, New
Jersey. Being pregnant again I was sick and
tired a lot, and I fell asleep on the couch every
time I tried to read aloud to the boys.

One afternoon I fell asleep while the boys scrambled all
over me, knocking an electric candle in the bay window onto
the couch. I slept until it started melting, filling the room
with smoke. It wasn't a fire—those would come later—but
the smoke woke me up. Pregnancy with three little boys was
hard. It was a dark and dreary house, and I hated it. We had
lived in houses with roaches and mice and fleas but dark and
dreary was the worst.

Then, one day, we saw an ad for a blue house in the country with a pond, a few acres, a greenhouse, and a chicken
coop. I begged God for this house. I paced and prayed and

pleaded. I tried not to let the landlord see that I was pregnant because he wasn't sure he wanted to rent to a family with children, and we had three so far plus the not-so-well-hidden baby bump. In the end, he decided we were okay and he rented the house to us. Eventually, I had three more babies in that blue house. God was good, and Bob just laughed.

While in labor, I walked during the contractions and rested in between. I ran towards the roar, and it worked. Walking did not cut down on the pain, but I felt like I might outrun it. I paced the floor of our home in a circle: kitchen, dining room, living room, porch. My new midwife, Mrs. Riley, who would go on to deliver my next five babies, was a mother of ten. She was silver-haired and strong-minded. You don't have ten kids without developing a tough hide.

I was beginning to adapt to going through labor. In the early years, I stuck to my Lamaze breathing, but as time went on I began to almost resent it. In fact, I resented my husband when he tried to get me to breathe. Poor guy, he had to put up with a lot from me when I was in labor. He never complained except for the time when I bit his shoulder during Nathaniel's birth. We are still at an impasse on that one: he thinks I should not have done it but I think he deserved it for obvious reasons. Tim was such a wonderful labor companion, though, that I could not imagine giving birth without his support and often worried he would die before the baby was born. He walked with me and played cards and understood when I didn't want to breathe anymore. I also figured out that it was imperative to wait for the urge to push and not rush it. That takes incredible discipline, and often I would just pretend that I felt the urge to push because transition was unbearable. Sticking out transition for just a few extra minutes can make a huge difference in the final stages of a birth. Even though I say that, I can still remember the bitterness, even anger, I felt whenever my midwife would say, "Just a few more minutes, Cindy, and you will be holding your baby." In transition, a few more minutes seems an eternity.

Sometime in the first hours of that early March morning with GLAD singing a capella on the cassette player and crocuses blooming on the lawn, Nathaniel was born. He was a gift from God.

I decided to "schedule" this baby for my sanity because I had been told it was more spiritual to schedule a baby. And if there was one thing I wanted to be it was spiritual. Stubbornly, I stuck it out, in spite of his tears, until I fed him solids at eight months. When I finally gave him enough to eat, he became the happiest little boy on earth for a few years. I would never again try to schedule a baby, although I would continue to make many mistakes in the name of spirituality.

I received an unusual baby gift when Nathaniel was born. My sister-in-law, Nancy, gave me the complete six-volume set of Charlotte Mason's *Original Home School Series*, a set still sitting on my shelf, though now a couple of the volumes are falling apart from being read and re-read. I was just beginning my homeschool journey, and little did I realize I already had everything I needed. It would have saved me a lot of money if I had known that the right philosophy is the greater part of the battle.

Now we had four little boys, and homeschooling began in earnest. We ordered our days according to school and nature walks and fishing.

Then Timothy and I developed a new obsession when, one day, we heard about a library sale in town. We had never been to one before. With great joy we scoured the tables for books like the ones Gladys Hunt talked about in *Honey for a Child's Heart,* a book I had almost memorized. We came home with bags and boxes of beautiful finds and a new hobby. For the next ten years or so our ever pressing need would be more bookshelves. And we had to learn to be aggressive. Those book sales were competitive with people pushing and shoving to be the first ones through the doors when they opened; sometimes people even grabbed books right out of our hands.

Just last year, as I found myself once again scouring the tables of our annual library book sale, I noticed that it wasn't so competitive anymore. Across the tables from me were only two old homeschooling moms, and none of us had any business buying books. Perhaps we should have been at some twelve-step meeting for book-buying addicts instead. Nevertheless, my calendar was still marked with this year's sale which turned into a book buying party with most of our local Charlotte Mason homeschoolers, many of whom are quite young. So instead of buying too many books for myself I was able to suggest books to other moms. I think this is called enabling.

But the boys and I weren't just buying books, we were trying to read them all, too.

In the mornings, after reviewing Timothy's Bible verse and acting out a few nursery rhymes, we would settle into a read aloud. Then we would go fishing, eat lunch, nap, and read again. Sometimes we would take a nature walk, picking up things to draw when we got home. These were happy, happy days. No pressure. No tests. Just the boys and I playing, reading, walking, and fishing. I eventually bought a hands-on math curriculum to jazz things up, but the older boys were never all that enamored with math manipulatives. Mostly we remember the reading.

Looking back, I realized that I was reading some pretty hefty stuff to this little five-year-old boy and the even littler guys who were always hovering in the background. But they hung in there, and I am pretty sure at least Timothy remembers these books as well as I do.

Of all the books, over all the years, these are the ones I remember most.

We read many Signature Biographies which astounds me now because they were not written for five-year-olds. Our favorites were *The Story of Dan Beard*, *The Story of Davy Crockett*, and *The Story of William Penn*.

We were lucky to find some of the *We Were There* books at the library sales. These books are a little like G.A. Henry books, placing a fictional character in the middle of historical events. In the 1940s and 1950s, publishers in America were getting the best authors to write children's historical books. It was a golden age in this genre and is unsurpassed since then.

We read *We Were There at the Battle of the Alamo*, and *We Were There at the Battle of Gettysburg*.

We went through a Marguerite Henry phase that year, reading *King of the Wind: The Story of the Godolphin Arabian*; *Benjamin West and His Cat Grimalkin*; and *Justin Morgan Had a Horse*.

We read Howard Pyle and Laura Ingalls Wilder and

George McDonald. We read thirty-six of the greatest books in one year.

I was just as hungry for knowledge as Timothy was, so reading aloud was my way of catching up. That was our family's first time through *The Little House* series, a series I ended up reading four times. It was my first time reading *Robin Hood* and *Charlotte's Web* and *Caddie Woodlawn*. Looking back, I can hardly believe we read all those books. If I had not faithfully recorded it, I am sure I would have forgotten how many we read.

Now reading each title brings back a flood of memories. It is almost as if we lived in those books. We laughed and laughed through *Caddie Woodlawn*. We shivered through *The Long Winter*. We rode horses through the Arabian desert and ate donuts with Almanzo Wilder. We hunted with Dan Beard and learned to spell with Winston Churchill. We lived almost forty lives and died a few times, too. We remembered the Alamo with tears and escaped captivity with bravery.

When the boys went outside to play, I heard them say things like, "Look over yonder," and, "I need a blunderbuss." We read inside on the couch, cuddling close, and outside on a quilt near the garden. We read in the park and in the woods. We huddled in front of the heater in the winter and locked ourselves in the one air-conditioned room in the summer. We read and read and read and didn't even know we were doing it. We didn't check our email, or our phones, or turn on the television.

There was never any reason to call this kindergarten. If it was kindergarten, then I was in kindergarten, too. It was our life. We had no test at the end of the semester. The test is that we remember.

This reading was the seed of Morning Time, which is in some ways my claim to fame. Twenty-seven years ago Timothy and I got up in the morning and starting learning together. It is a funny name, Morning Time. It started, I guess, when I would call out in the mornings, "Ten minutes until Morning Time." The kids knew what that meant: In twenty minutes we would gather together.

Then, before we knew it, it was time to add another member to our mornings.

Nineteen months after Nathaniel was born, Christopher came along. He had a rough journey. Halfway through labor, we had to transfer to the hospital because of meconium in my water. My labor still lasted only three and a half hours, but a good portion of that was transition. He was turned funny. I sang "Jesus Loves Me," which turned out to be just the right breathing pattern. I had long ago given up Lamaze-type breathing in favor of walking through the contractions, and now I added singing. He didn't breathe right away, but when I reached out to touch him, he immediately let out a breath. He was over ten pounds, which my midwife blamed on the amount of milk I drank while pregnant. I would not make that mistake again.

That was a rough night; I was not a fan of hospitals. The nurse wore a necklace that said, "World's Best Mother." Someone loved her, but I did not. She kept rebuking me for how I was caring for Christopher. Why hadn't I changed his outfit in two hours? Why was I holding him so much? But I was not about to lose one second of those first magical moments in this little beloved human's life.

Some of my happiest memories are of Christopher in the bassinet in the living room during Morning Time. He cooed at the pictures of animals on the side of the bassinet while we read aloud. Sometimes he would pop his head up and look around at the rest of us and then go back to talking to his "friends."

Each day, we started Morning Time with prayer. I would write down the children's prayer requests so we could look back and see God's hand in our lives. We had one funny stretch where we were praying for our van door because the window had mysteriously broken when a ball hit it. We were also praying for a missionary family. Every morning someone would say, "We need to pray about the van door," and someone else would chime in, "and the Van Dorens."

Then we would read the Bible. We mostly read the Proverb of whatever calendar day it was (i.e., on the first day of the month we read Proverbs 1), or we read straight through the Bible from Genesis to Revelation. Then we would work on a memory verse from the Bible.

My college roommate had introduced me to a system of memorization that included reviewing things previously memorized. This system became the backbone of all our memory work. We would put a Bible verse on a 3x5 index card and read it every day for two weeks. After that, we added a new card. Each day we continued to read the card with our new verse, and we reviewed one old card on a rotating basis. That way we were continually reviewing past verses which solved the problem of forgetting what we had previously learned.

Soon we implemented a yearly field day, complete with

ribbons, awards, and ice cream. We still have the notebook full of our 'world' records. With so many different ages, the boys were generally competing against their own records, but it was a competition all the same, and they reveled in it.

One day when Nicholas was still quite small, he climbed about thirty feet to the top of a tree. Timothy ran in to tell us that Nicholas was up there and could not get down. We considered calling the fire department, but Tim decided to go up and get him. As they were nearing the bottom of the tree, Tim asked, "What is that vine clinging to the tree?" It was poison ivy. Within days, Nicholas looked like an alligator, as almost every part of his skin was covered in the rash, and Tim was wishing he had called the fire department.

Even though Tim worked long hours, he was almost always home when any of the boys got cut, or there was blood involved. I am notoriously unable to deal with blood. When I see a cut, my knees go weak, and I almost pass out. I have been known to run away from any child coming towards me to show me a bloody cut. When Tim wasn't home, Timothy had to deal with most of those injuries.

I probably used nap time more than most moms. I am often astounded by how few children take naps these days. I conned my children into taking naps until they were almost six, although James told me recently that he was an expert at making it looked like he had slept when he had not. He had a whole system for rubbing his eyes and rumpling his hair. It was hard for me to say, "go back to bed," if the child had apparently slept.

Things were getting crazy in the blue house. We were schooling in earnest now. And then I was pregnant again.

My favorite part of pregnancy was when that nesting urge started. I would frantically clean the house, especially the bathrooms. I tried to have a few cleaning ladies in over the years, but they always made me feel bad about myself. One girl stayed four hours, only finishing one bathroom. Another girl patted me on the head and said, "It's all right, honey." James says I forfeited the right to a clean house when I had eight boys, but that didn't keep me from trying.

I learned to compartmentalize rooms in our house. Out of sight, out of mind. The problem with this system was that when you finally checked a compartment, it was daunting. The boys had a huge attic room in the blue house, and I managed to avoid going up there much. I would ask them if it was clean and they would say, "Yes!" I was never prepared for just how messy "yes" was. When I would eventually go up there, I'd take one look at the room, lose my composure, and then sit down on the floor and cry. Then we would call off school for the day and all clean together. Christopher told me last year that when he was little Timothy taught him how to fold the top layer of clothing in the drawers while leaving the rest of the drawer a mess.

One day I found myself plowing full steam ahead through a dirty bathroom in preparation for another baby's birth. All the boys were helping me. Timothy, Nicholas, James, and Nathaniel were all there, working hard in our big bathroom. We were exhausted. When I finally looked up, I realized that toddler Christopher was not in there with us. No need to panic. Christopher was always wandering. We searched the house, but he was nowhere to be found. Soon we were panicking. Once he had tried crossing the street, and a lady from our church had brought him back to me. But the worst thing was the pond! I was terrified he would drown. The boys and I raced towards it as fast as we could go. They were quite a bit faster than me at nine months pregnant, and as James and Nathaniel neared the pond, they looked at the water and started wailing and pointing at the water. "Oh, no, oh, no, oh, no!!" They were howling. I ran as fast as I could. I got to the pond expecting to see Christopher floating in the water where they were pointing. It was the worst moment of my mothering career to date.

"Where is he? Where is he?" I screamed. They didn't know. They thought he might be in the water but had not seen him there and were worried about him. We headed back to our house, but Nicholas said, "Let me go and check the woods." To my relief, within minutes, Nicholas emerged from the woods with baby Christopher. The sight of the boys pointing at the pond and crying is etched in my mind as if Christopher really had been floating there.

Then, all of a sudden, the next labor started even as a hurricane ripped up the coast near us. I began the walk: kitchen, living room, dining room, porch. How did I get myself into labor again? I asked myself, as the pain became more and more intense. Then we had Benjamin, born during a storm. He was one of the most beautiful babies I had ever seen. It was one of my easiest labors, and he was my sixth son. I was starting to think maybe we would only have boys. I began to worry that I would mess up a girl.

I added things to our Morning Time on a regular basis. We were at church one Wednesday night in the fellowship hall when our pastor announced a hymn. There were no hymn books, and so we all began to sing by heart. I had been in church my whole life, but I only knew the first verse of "My Hope is Built on Nothing Less" by Edward Mote, and I noted that our pastor's children, who were older than mine and also homeschooled, knew all the words of all the verses. By the end of verse four, their family was singing alone. I was jealous. I felt competitive. I wanted my kids to know all the words to all the hymns, too. I wanted to win the hymn contest, and so Thursday morning, the day after prayer meeting, we began learning hymns, in the same way we were learning Bible verses. We would sing the first verse of a hymn every day for one week. Week two we would sing verses one and two, and so on. Then, after we had learned all the verses to a hymn, it would go in the review pile. Each morning we would sing a new hymn, verse by verse, and review an old hymn, all the verses. I was a bit neurotic about learning all the verses. Now I know that is called self-righteousness.

It turns out that no matter what your motivation for learning hymns, there are many benefits. The first benefit is that you can sing even before you can read, or when you are holding two babies or when, God forbid, you are nursing a baby in church. Hymn memorization is hands-free.

I also believe looking at a hymnal helps children learn to read if they already know the words. Some children get excited that they are singing along with the hymn book. Plus, knowing hymns helps children engage and participate in church. I think that is one reason a traditional liturgy is helpful. You know what is coming and what is expected, and, therefore, you can take part.

Learning all the verses can be a wonderful lesson in theology. I am known to get annoyed with music leaders who say, "Verses one, two, and four," when it is evident that verse three is the heart and soul of the hymn. How can you skip:

*"My sin, oh the bliss of this glorious thought! My sin, not in part but the whole. Is nailed to the cross, and I bear it no more, Praise the Lord, Praise the Lord, oh, my soul."*

Of course, it is true that in some hymnals "The Church's One Foundation" has over twenty verses. I am not so hard-nosed as I used to be. Eleven verses are fine.

The Bible encourages us to learn Psalms and hymns and spiritual songs, and when we are alone and in dark places, those words are often the things to which our hearts tune. There truly are ten thousand reasons for our hearts to sing.

You should sing whether your family sounds good or not. After two of our better singers graduated, the younger children would quickly shut the windows when it came time to sing each morning. My husband has a tender ear and he sometimes cringed to hear us, but that was no reason not to sing. When I did finally get discouraged enough to quit singing with my children, two of my musical friends separately and gently rebuked me. It was wrong for us not to sing because we didn't sound lovely. We should still make a joyful noise. So back to singing badly we went.

Recently, I taught my little granddaughters, Anabella and Savanna, to sing "In the Bleak Midwinter." I could hear my aging voice crack and quiver, but I persevered nonetheless. They will never say their CiCi had a good voice, but I hope they will always remember, "In the bleak midwinter, frosty wind made moan. Earth stood hard as iron, water like a stone...." I am counting on those hauntingly beautiful lyrics by Christina Georgina Rossetti to endure in their hearts. Maybe someday they will teach them to their granddaughters.

I like to think that Bible memory and hymn-singing will last into eternity because they are based on praise.

My motivation to learn hymns was not spiritual, but the fruit we have borne as a family is. God works in mysterious ways His wonders to perform.

Then came a new period in our life: It was time to buy a house. We had six children and more to come. What kind of house should we buy?

Tim and I sat down with a friend of ours and evaluated ourselves as honestly as we could. We knew that we should buy a newer house that didn't need too many repairs. Tim worked long hours and didn't have time for household jobs. We clearly understood this. Surely, we understood this!

But the next day we looked at a farm on eight acres. It was as old as any house in New Jersey could be. In fact, it may have been *the oldest* house in New Jersey. The owner just said, "Paint and plaster cover a multitude of sins."

But paint and plaster do not cover human sins. This was the house where Tim and I would find out what we were made of. It turns out we were made of some pretty sad stuff.

CHAPTER FOUR

# Intery, Mintery, Cuttery Corn

*"One flew East, one flew West,*
*one flew over the cuckoo's nest."*
**Traditional Nursery Rhyme**

*A*s we searched for houses to buy we clearly understood our limitations. We spoke them out loud. But within twenty-four hours of acknowledging them, we were throwing this knowledge away to buy a tumbled-down old farm on eight New Jersey acres.

We moved to the farm as a family of six boys: four of them rascals, one a wandering toddler, and one a baby. We would leave five years later with eight children, one of them our precious daughter. The first two years were somewhat hopeful; we were going to reclaim this home and farm. The next three years began with a gradual awakening to the fact that we were not improving the farm and most likely never would. A sort of darkness descended over my heart.

The farmhouse was a series of three houses: Two large

ancient farmhouses, each with different levels smashed together with shared attics, plus an even older cheese house. Outbuildings dotted the property, including an ivy-covered outhouse tilting precariously with its half-moon door cutout. Rows of milking stanchions filled the biggest barn. But none of that is why we bought the farm. We bought it because it had a huge garage building with a large workshop. Somebody in our family loved the workshop, and somebody else had romantic ideas about farm life. At first it had a tractor, but the former owner took it away after a few months. That was when we began the tag team lawn mowing of the acreage with the push mower. We mowed all summer long, all day long, each family member taking his turn, including me.

Even so, our first farm Thanksgiving was wonderful. We ate in the Cheese House, which was probably the original structure, heating it via the old cookstove set in the chimney. We covered the walls with quilts (I have quite a collection from my grandmothers and great aunts) and the rafters with herbs from our garden. Friends and family from out of town arrived to feast with us. It flurried outside, and we were cold, but it was magical. For the first time in our marriage, we were homeowners.

One Christmas we bought a horse. His name was Freckles because he was pale and freckled and he was what was called 'green broke,' only we didn't know that. Obviously. We weren't in the habit of buying horses; we just read books about horses. Freckles was uncontrollably antsy, something about his feed and his evil personality. But Timothy and Nicholas were fearless. They would mount Freckles along the side of the pen and he would run to a nearby field, throw them, and gallop around the neighborhood for hours. For some unknown reason, he always came home again. Sometimes he would throw them and then stand there waiting for them to remount. As they would put one leg over his back, he would quit waiting. It hurt to have a horse. Eventually, we gave him to a local farm family in exchange for riding lessons for all the older boys. Nobody ever rode Freckles.

We also had cats to keep the mice at bay. Every day we had more cats, and none of us liked cats at all. We kept chickens, and because we had chickens we had rats. As it turned out, rats were my limit. I could not love my family if I lived in a house with rats. The rats were like demons stealing my sanity away. At first we did not know they were there. They didn't get caught or scratch or squeal like mice. They just snuck in and ate the food. The only evidence they left behind was a stray hair or two and huge bites in the food. The whole family started a conspiracy to keep me from knowing about them.

But since the rats made me crazy I put up with the ever-growing number of cats. The cat community started growing this way: A friend gave us a cat, and one day that cat was in a chest of drawers on top of someone's clothes with two babies, so that was three cats and a life lesson on shutting your drawers. The cats came in the house, but I didn't mind because as long as they were there, rodents must beware. My husband complained that the cats ate birds, which he loved. But my sanity was wavering. Who cared if they ate birds as long as they scared rats and ate mice?

One day we watched one of the cats give birth, which was exciting except for the part where we had sixteen cats wandering around.

Once, I looked down, and there was a mole at my feet. He had dug his way up through my floorboards, the ones laying directly on the earth. Another day I looked up, and there was a snake over my washer. Tim opened the door to the washer tub and knocked the snake in with a broom. I didn't mind the snake so much because snakes eat rats, but the rest of the family was scared stiff. I think it was a spiritual problem. They even killed black snakes out of fear. I laughed at black snakes. The boys were so terrified of black snakes that they couldn't even kill them decently with a hoe. Instead, they grabbed a shotgun and blasted them into hyperspace.

At Christmas, the mice crawled up our Christmas tree, nibbling the popcorn and cranberries. Our neighbor babysitter found this charming. She wrote a poem about our Christmas mouse. Meanwhile, the boys shot at the mice (on the Christmas tree, in the house) with a bb gun. What was worse, so did Tim. I was just happy it wasn't the shotgun.

Then there were the bats. I opened a window one day when I saw something squished between the panes. Two little bats were curled up sleeping, looking all the world like what they really were--rats with wings. Then there was the night the boys and Tim stayed up all night trying to capture bats in the living room. Their weapons of choice were tennis rackets. I stayed in my room because I had long hair and everyone knows if a bat gets in your hair you have to shave your head. I have known that since I was ten.

We kept all of our extra clothes in the attics which were held together by numbered beams and wood pins. It was fresh and woody up there, except for the wasps. I had to quit going up there because I had not developed the art of standing still until the wasp got bored with me. The boys would yell at me, "Just be still, Mama!" But I couldn't do it. I would run and scream and flail. And, yet, I have never in my life been stung by a wasp. As still as they kept, I do believe the boys were stung now and then.

Then there was all the "stuff."

I was proud of my system of organizing out-of-season clothes. When you have a large family of mostly one sex, you have a lot of clothing items because every family with boys from miles around will automatically think of you when they have hand-me-downs. At first, this will be helpful, and your guys will always look snazzy at church, but later it will grow into a monster of unimaginable proportions worthy of its own private landfill.

So I bought see-through plastic bins and numbered them. Then I had a notebook with an index and a page for each bin. I recorded what was in the bin and put it in the attic. The boys would put the containers away and get them out according to which number I wanted. It was an efficient system for a large family.

The boys seemed invincible. Since our house had at least seven levels, it was easy to escape me. I worried about Christopher, the wanderer. There was a chance that if he went up one set of stairs and down another and I went a different way, we would never see each other again. But with five other helpers, we could usually cut him off at one pass or another.

We had a huge old upright piano, and one day I wanted it moved up a level. I do not know how they did it, but Timothy and Nicholas, twelve and ten, picked up that giant piano and hoisted it up to the next level. Truly, they were mighty boys.

We also had hawks that stalked our chickens. One day, after we had been living there for a while, I put my baby girl, Emily, who was born at the farm, in a laundry basket while I hung the wash (hanging wash outside in the breeze was my therapy). Suddenly, a huge hawk swooped down right over Emily, inches away from her. I could feel his flapping wings beating, their wind touching my face. It was a frightening moment, but he barely avoided her, realizing she was not a chicken, I guess.

Spring on the farm was beautiful. We had lilacs and peonies which made up for much. Rats and sins and paint and plaster and critters and husbands were all forgiven when the blossoms were on the apples, the ornamental cherry flaunted itself outside the kitchen window, and lilacs and peonies graced our table. One sprig of lilac in a vase can transform the drabbest environment. Timothy and I put in two or three magnificent gardens, and I developed my philosophy of gardening. In the summer, we planted sunflowers in rows, and we would have flocks of goldfinches flitting through the yard. Vegetables were easy to come by and cheap in the summer. Every farmer for miles around dropped zucchini on our front porch. Flowers were much more rare. More and more of my garden space was taken up with them. I had a white moonlight garden, a dried flower garden, an herb garden, a cutting flower garden, and a butterfly section. I cannot see why anyone would plant zucchini when they could plant larkspur.

And always, in the background, calming my heart, was the music. Timothy had learned to play the piano. At first, he had a teacher who taught him all of the chords. He had an uncanny ear. He could play any tune after hearing it once. Eventually, we found a stricter teacher who was not impressed with his ear shenanigans. She made him discipline himself. It was the perfect combination. I would fall asleep almost every night listening to Timothy playing the piano down the hall. I would almost be willing to go back to the farm to hear that music once again.

§

It was a lot of work taking care of eight children, three tumble-down houses, and a menagerie of animals.

It didn't take long for us to realize we were living in too many centuries. Tim went to work in the Twentieth Century, keeping long hours. He came home to the Eighteenth Century. In the Eighteenth Century, his family was chopping wood to keep somewhat warm. His family was eating a big pot of oatmeal every morning heated on the wood stove. His family was trying to care for dogs and cats and horses and chickens in possibly the oldest house in New Jersey.

I could have written this chapter two different ways. One way would have sounded pretty neat. I had read books like that before we bought the farm—Gladys Tabor and Stillmeadow and all that. I could have talked about the day the boys woke up from sleeping in the cheese house attic with snow on their blankets, just like in *The Long Winter*. I could tell you about their romps under the farm floors, and up in the barn rafters, only I didn't know about those at the time. How are the boys still alive? I can't write this chapter the way I imagined it would be. I was not Hannah Coulter. The farm of our dreams was just that: a fantasy. We had fallen for a dream sequence in some homeschool guru's repertoire.

On the other hand, the boys seemed to thrive. They loved chopping wood to heat our home even though it was a never-ending job. It is deeply satisfying to a boy's heart to hack at logs. Just yesterday Andrew came to me and said, "If you buy wood, I will chop it." We don't heat our home with wood (or even use it anymore except for bonfires), but Andrew will chop it for the sheer manly joy of it.

One day I saw something utterly gross in the pantry. I don't remember exactly what it was but something snapped in my mind that day. It was  gross and white and squiggly and it was the end for me. I walked out the back door and into the apple orchard—the pretty, pretty apple orchard pretending to offer a way of life long gone—and laid down under the ancient apple tree and cried loudly. I was never going to make it in the Eighteenth Century. I was disappointed in myself and my husband. I blamed him for the grossness in the pantry.  He blamed me for blaming him. It was going to take us a long time to get out of this mess. Knowing we weren't self-sufficient, we knew it was time to move. The farm had broken us, our marriage was not in good shape, and we were disappointed in our dream and each other. Thankfully, we were still committed to our trust in Christ and our belief in the institution of marriage. Our marriage would weather this storm and heal.

So we put the farm on the market. But who would buy it? Only a crazy person. It was hard for me to keep it clean and straight with so many children, but one day a couple came to the door unannounced. Could they look at the house? I so desperately wanted to sell it that I said yes. I nodded to Timothy, and he got my message. While I slowly wound the couple through the labyrinthian house, the boys spread out cleaning rooms ahead of me. When I finally got to one bedroom and opened the closet, there was a boy smashed up against the back wall trying to be inconspicuous. At least the closet was clean. But those people were not crazy and so they did not buy it. The person who finally bought the farm could only be called a hoarder. He bought the place to have room to store his vast collection of junk. The huge barns and outbuildings were perfect for him. He may have been crazy, but I love that man so much.

The Farm was a long time ago now, but I still get a bit shaky when I see pictures of it. In my mind, there is always a rat photobombing my memories. I will never be able to own chickens again, and that is sad, because chickens are so much fun.

The Farm introduced me to my limitations, which were much more profound than I imagined. The issue wasn't that I had limitations, because, of course, I did. The real problem was that I had never imagined them. Now my eyes were opened: I had endured giving birth to so many children, but I was not invincible.

# CHAPTER FIVE

# The Old Woman Who Lived in a Shoe

*"Though this be madness, yet there is method in't."*
**William Shakespeare**

*W*hile we were facing the overwhelming difficulties of farm life, we were also experiencing some of life's other ups and downs.

In the midst of the chaos of our Eighteenth Century farm life, I found out I was pregnant again. I stared at the baby pictures on the mantle in my bedroom and wondered how I could endure another labor. I had an ultrasound but asked that they not tell me the sex of the baby. The ultrasound was tinted pink; I wondered about it a little, then put it out of my mind.

But one morning, my water finally broke. We called Mrs. Riley, our midwife, and the walk of doom began.

We were having a home birth in April in New Jersey, in a house heated solely with wood. The boys' job was to keep the house warm during the birth. They faithfully brought in stacks of wood and fed the stove with as much wood as it would hold, continually stoking it. By the time I felt the urge to push, the house was boiling. Later, the boys said they knew it was a girl by all the screaming upstairs. We named her Emily. She was perfection, but I was terrified. What if I ruined her? We had been in so many churches with so many ideas about the roles of women, I didn't know where to begin. In some ways, boys were just boys. They were a force. They were going to grow up and be men somehow, but this little pink bundle seemed so fragile. I prayed over and over again that she would not be my idea of a godly woman, or some church's idea, or some guru's prairie muffin, but that she would grow up to be God's idea of a Christian woman. The first differences between Emily and the boys were noticeable when she was just a few days old: She would try to coo and participate in conversations. She was much more verbally active. I enjoyed dressing her up, but I often found my favorite dresses for her were not pink but blue. I loved buying her old-fashioned prairie dresses too, in spite of my prayer.

At that time, I only wore dresses. It is hard to see how this evolved. It was a gradual change; one I barely noticed happening until dresses were all I wore. It made sledding and horseback riding difficult, but I stuck to my ideals. Perhaps it was the sheer difficulty of finding clothes when I wore several different sizes a year due to pregnancy and nursing. Dresses were a simple choice. Jumpers were in style and easy to find; add a pair of white Keds and the homeschool mom uniform was complete. It did have one significant drawback. It was easier to gain weight while wearing loose dresses. I had no skinny jeans to squeeze into, so my weight blossomed with my dresses.

During these years I loved to dress the children in matching clothes, often polo shirts and khakis. I remember the very last time I got away with this. It was Easter Sunday, right after Emily's birth. My mom had bought the six boys bright yellow polos for church. As they sat in the pew a lady behind squealed, "Look at all the yellow duckies." In unison Timothy and Nicholas turned and glared at me. I knew it was the last time they would match.

Then, when Emily was about nine months old, another trauma burdened us. I had an unusual mole on my shoulder, and my doctor suggested I see a dermatologist. I made an appointment but ended up missing it. I decided not to reschedule, but I could not stop thinking about it. I was anti-doctor in those days but for some reason, I rescheduled the appointment. Around Christmas, the news came back, "You have melanoma." I went home and pulled out my medical book. It said something like, "Melanoma is one of the deadliest cancers. The survival rate for fourth stage melanoma is 5%. Melanoma patients do not waste away but die quickly."

Great. I had battled my weight my whole life and now I couldn't even get a disease where I would waste away.

For two weeks, we waited to hear what stage I was in. The survival rate for stage one was 95%, but after that, it dropped dramatically. It was a tense two weeks. I had always thought I didn't care whether I lived or died, especially with the rats, but now I found myself longing to live. My health food co-op friends suggested I juice to fight the cancer. I asked Tim if we could buy a juicer in order to save my life. He reminded me we could not chase every fad around in order to beat cancer;

we didn't have an unlimited budget. I agreed, but thought maybe my life was worth more than the small amount the juicer would cost. In the end it worked out. I wasn't all that fond of apple juice and spinach water.

In the midst of the blizzard of '96 I went to the University of Pennsylvania to have the melanoma removed. It took five hours. I know this because they could not give me general anesthesia since I was still nursing baby Emily. I lay on the operating table with the clock directly in front of me. The fraction of an ounce of skin they removed left a huge scar down my shoulder. It was not quite stage two; I was probably going to live. This should have made me happy, but for some reason, I could not shake off the feeling that after all those years of feeling so passionate and purposeful, God didn't need me after all. It was quite a comeuppance. I struggled to make sense of my purpose now that I did not feel indispensable.

This pity party went on for a while until one day I was reading the parable of the talents in Matthew 25. In that story, a man goes on a journey, entrusting his servants with different amounts of money. One servant receives five talents, another two, and another one. The first two servants invest their talents, which pleases their master, but the servant with only one talent doesn't invest the money, but buries it. When his master calls him to account he says something similar to what I was feeling: "Master, I knew you to be a hard man, reaping where you did not sow, and gathering where you scattered no seed, so I was afraid, and I went and hid your talent in the ground. Here you have what is yours."

Because I realized during the melanoma scare that God

didn't "need" me, I had lost my passion for life. I immediately recognized my folly and repented, eventually regaining my passion and zeal for living.

That was twenty years ago. I still have annual checkups and our whole family has what is called 'weird moles,' but I am thankful for the last twenty years; they were a gift.

As homeschooling became more complicated with so many glitches, hardships, and moves, I started streamlining our days. I made sure that we were having Morning Time and that the boys were doing math, a written narration, and reading for two to three hours each day. Housework, farm chores, and the constant stream of farming neighbors who needed a 'boy' for the day helped all this add up to a decent education.

With my health deteriorating and the miscarriages multiplying, it looked like we might not have any more children. But then, one happy day, I found out I was pregnant again.

Nine months later, Andrew was born. Apparently, we had not been just trying for the girl. My midwife delivered him at the hospital, and he was induced three weeks before his due date. He was born exactly ten years, to the hour, after his brother James, on the Ides of March. Andrew was a delightful baby from the get-go. He loved to cuddle. Most of my babies, even Emily, cuddled until they gained the slightest mobility and then they were raring to get going, but Andrew stuck around a little longer. I was getting older and no longer panicked about how many children I might have, so I was able to relax and enjoy nursing and holding him. It was a special time in my life, and he was a special baby for all of us. The farm was a rough place to live, but Andrew was a beautiful child.

§

When we left the farm, we rented a three-story federal brick house on an estate. This brought us into the Nineteenth Century. Our new place, wedged between farm fields, was only one hundred and fifty years old. It was a haven of rest for me.

Into this haven, we brought one more baby, one last blessing to end my childbearing years. When I had my ultrasound, this time, the nurses asked me what we had already. I said we had seven boys and a girl. They looked forlorn. One of them said, "We are so sorry, honey, we will give you some privacy to deal with the fact that you are having another boy." I just laughed. What did I care whether it was a boy or a girl? It was my last baby. We ended our childbearing years with Alex, a little fellow much like our firstborn son. He was born at St. Francis Hospital in Wilmington, DE. I am not Catholic, but I praise the Lord for the Catholic hospitals across this country which celebrate life. Every once in a while, a little bell rang throughout the hospital, and when I asked the nurse what it was she said it meant a baby had been born. When a visitor asked me if I was finally going to have my tubes tied, a nurse piped in, "We don't do that here." I am not against birth control, but I am for life. Catholic hospitals deserve all of our support in these days when life is so disrespected.

Before Alex was born, I began to have increasing panic attacks thinking about going through labor and delivery. I had birthed my first eight children 'naturally', forgoing even a stitch of pain medication. I wanted my babies to be born alert and able to nurse. I was afraid an epidural would spoil that. But eventually, my fear of labor took over.

When I went to the hospital in labor with Alex, I immediately asked to see the anesthesiologist. He said, "Why do you want pain meds after having eight babies without them?" The guy tried to talk me out of them. I looked at him and said, "Seriously? I want pain meds because I have had eight babies naturally." Then I had to explain to the anesthesiologist that my labors were quick, and I needed the meds before I reached three centimeters. He finally agreed, but he must not have given me much because an hour later I was in a lot of pain. My husband complained to the nurse, and she brought me an oral drug. I thought I would hate the drowsy feeling, but it felt pleasant. The anesthesiologist came back and gave me another zap, and I was finally pain-free. When it came time to push, in spite of the drugs, I knew. The machine said otherwise. I insisted. The nurse checked and then ran for the doctor. Tim almost got to deliver Alex while the nurse ran to get the doctor. To my relief, Alex was alert and responsive after all those drugs and I would never be an obnoxious mother-in-law bragging that I had ALL my babies naturally.

The end of pregnancy was always an intense time for me as I struggled to prepare my nest. I got upset and yelled at the boys more often during those final weeks of pregnancy and I wondered if Alex was thinking while I cooed at him sweetly after he was born, "Who is this lady? My mom doesn't sound this sweet."

I am not sure Alex ever cried more than a few seconds. No, I am not exaggerating. I could never bear to hear a baby cry and none of my older children could either. My older boys became experts at calming distressed infants. I had to fight to even hold Alex. With nine other people clamoring for a chance, my only opportunity came when he was hungry. On more than one occasion, I put Alex down for a nap only to look up a few minutes later to see someone carrying him around. "I heard him crying," was their excuse. Our whole family loved Andrew and Alex excessively. We all sensed they were the end of the line, and now that we were out of the stress of the farmhouse, all the joy we could muster fell on them.

In 1983, Tim and I were on the verge of undergoing fertility diagnostics. In 2001, we had our sixteenth pregnancy and our ninth child. Sometimes life is unpredictable. Once, a pastor's wife said to me, "Because you have a large family, you will have much joy and much pain in life."

While I was never one to enjoy being pregnant and I often feared labor and delivery, the highlight of my life has been those nine times I got to hold my sweet newborns. Babies are usually alert for the first few hours, looking around with pure wonder. To be the person who gets to look back into their eyes is a precious gift. The bond I formed with those children in those wee hours is unbreakable. Perhaps it was excessive to have nine children. My friend was right. I have had joy, and I have had much pain, too. Eleven sinners in one home can create a lot of grief. But I can never forget those first hours when I became friends with the nine persons I call my babies.

Throughout all the turmoil of the farm and moving, we continued to homeschool, and we continued to have Morning Time. Before we started Morning Time each day, we had morning meeting. That was the time I used to talk about our schedules for the day. As the boys grew older, this meeting became increasingly important as we all shared two vehicles. When the older boys had to go somewhere, they used our white fifteen-passenger van. This was not sexy, they often told us.

I also used our morning meetings to discuss things like hygiene, household rules, and daily logistics. I would say, "Raise your hand if you brushed your teeth?" In spite of the fact that I asked this question day after day, year after year, the usual response was dismal. You could almost say my system had trained them not to brush their teeth.

Our mornings had the same routine for over twenty years. Wake up, make your bed, read your Bible, eat breakfast, brush your teeth, do your chore, start your math, come to Morning Time.

I learned to assign permanent chores rather than using any rotating or chart system. If I had had a chart, my life would have revolved around holding the kids responsible for it. Permanent jobs simplified our life. A child assigned to the dishes might do them for years. In fact, for years, I rarely touched a dirty dish (although, these days I am back at it). It might have seemed like I was lazy for requiring the kids to do all the housework, but the minute I took time out to work on the house, all hell broke loose somewhere else. My job was to patrol and admonish. It was a tough job.

As you can imagine, we had mountains of dirty laundry. Early on we stopped even talking about the 'laundry;' I would just say, 'rotate.' That meant Benjamin, if it was his job, had to start a load of wash, put a load in the dryer, fold all the clothes, and put them away. For maybe fifteen years we never, ever caught up on the laundry; we just kept rotating. The good news is that 'rotating' also kept us from getting too far behind. To fall behind on the laundry in a large family is truly a disaster.

Then there were the socks. How do you sort socks for eight boys? My mother was always coming up with ingenious schemes to sort the socks. "Maybe the boys could pretend their socks were knights…." My poor mom, she could never understand my system. Buy only white socks for all boys. Keep all the socks in one large laundry basket. Never sort them. It was easy enough for the boys to find what they needed that way. If I had sorted socks, then that would have been my whole life. Same with underwear. Sure, sometimes the ten year-old squeezed into the 2T underwear, and often the toddler's underwear sagged, but that was better than a life devoted to sorting.

You may think this simplification of life was unnecessary, but with nine children no amount of simplification is too much.

In fact, one of our sons turned twelve twice. When what we thought was his thirteenth birthday rolled around we had to sadly explain to him that he going to have to be twelve again since we had miscalculated his last birthday. This was a crushing blow.

§

I loved reading aloud to the children, but I struggled to homeschool so many students. The happy days of no-pressure kindergarten were long past. Every year, I had a new student. I was teaching several children to read at the same time, and I was tossed to-and-fro on waves of different methods. My friends were using everything from Konos to Tapestry of Grace, Unschooling to the Principle Approach. Classical education was becoming popular with its idea of ages-and-stages. I was perpetually confused. I finally felt crazy enough that I decided to buy a curriculum entirely based on workbooks. All we had to do was get up every day and pull out the workbooks. It should have been easy, but it wasn't. At the end of the year, we hadn't made it through even a third of the workbooks, and what's more, we hadn't read aloud as much and we had skipped Morning Time altogether.

That summer, I had an x-ray on my lungs because, with melanoma, the lungs are vulnerable. And there it was—a mass. The melanoma was going to get me after all. Why in the world was I trying to make the kids do workbooks when I should be curled up on the couch talking and reading with them? All those minutes from the last year were gone, and all we had were three workbooks filled in per child. There weren't even the usual stack of written narrations. It looked like my time was running out.

In a twinkling—I can still see the place in my house where I was standing—I decided to go back to Morning Time, even if it meant giving up a sense of accomplishment. Morning Time, I was beginning to realize, is not for today like a workbook is. It is for the long haul. As it turned out, it was only a shadow on my X-Ray, a providential shadow that woke me up in the midst of a terrible mistake.

That same summer we finally began to read Shakespeare.

We spent that midsummer reading *A Midsummer Night's Dream* in the backyard, and I will always remember my surprise when the children laughed in the right places. Then I heard about something that would eventually be called Ambleside Online, a program dedicated to developing a modern, free version of Charlotte Mason's own Parents' Union schools. I was ready to go the long haul.

# CHAPTER SIX

# All's Right with the World

*"The question is not how much does the youth know when he has finished his education but how much does he care?"*
**Charlotte Mason**

orning Time was back in full swing and would stay that way. When confronted with something I couldn't find time for in our regular school days, I started to ask myself, "Can I do this in Morning Time?"

From the beginning, we read poetry during Morning Time. I had always read nursery rhymes to the children, but I also owned an old leather-covered poetry volume, One-Hundred and One Famous Poems, given to me by my much-loved grandmother. Her book was my treasure. In fact, she was the only person whom I ever allowed to read my poems in high school, poems I burned in a fit of hormones, thank goodness. Her little book was always by my side, and so it was quite natural for me to pick it up and start reading it aloud to the children in the morning. I am not saying those poems rose to the level of great poetry because many of them did not, but they were accessible, which is what made them famous (starting your first-grade student on "The Second Coming" by Yeats is probably not a good idea). Most of our early poetry memorizationcame from this book. The second poem is the one I quote the most, "Opportunity," by Edward R. Sill. Has there ever been a better verse for boys? The boys also loved "Keep 'A Goin' " by Frank Stanton, "How Did You Die" by Edmund Vance Cook, and the memorial "The Charge of the Light Brigade" by Alfred, Lord Tennyson.

Often I hear mothers worry that poetry is a feminine pursuit. If you wonder how poetry can grow a man, I will tell you.

*"Half a league, half a league, Half a league onward . . ."*

So starts one of the most famous poems in English Literature. Famous, yes, and these days debunked. What is the use of an old worn-out Tennyson poem full of jingoistic and even dangerous sentiment?

In preparation for a talk I gave once, I went over years and years of school papers and thought quite a bit about the hours and hours of Morning Time I spent with my family. I wondered if I was romanticizing the whole thing.

I asked Benjamin, who struggled with memorization, if he ever used the poems we learned. He said that he had learned to retrieve it from his mind when he was training to run a marathon a few years ago. He was running with his oldest brother and noticed how Timothy quoted Bible verses, poems, and songs while pushing through a run. Benjamin said, "I don't remember all the words but I especially like to say the poem about 'half a league, half a league' and 'theirs not to not to make reply.' " So he and I recited it together and he did well.

You might think this is a pretty poor showing for years and years of memory work, but then again, Dorothy Sayers claims that in spite of years of Latin she didn't really know the language. What was the use of that? What I mean is, if you can't assess something then there must not be any value in it, right?

And yet, at least two of my sons quoted Tennyson when running marathons, and Dorothy Sayers created Lord Peter Wimsey, the perfect man.

And then something else happened which made me love Tennyson and his poetry. I have a bit of an addiction to BBC television, and Amazon Prime suggested I try *London Hospital*. The reviews were good, so I jumped in. In one episode a British laborer is injured while putting others first in a life-threatening situation. He is a hero but he loses both legs. While dealing with the ensuing pain, this uneducated man starts trying to say "The Charge of the Light Brigade" and the nurse joins in. Then so do I (and not without tears) and all the while I am thinking, that is why we read poetry. That is why we have Morning Time!

That is a romantic story, and "The Charge of the Light Brigade" is a romantic poem, and I have, indeed, romanticized Morning Time. And that, my friend, is the point. There is not a poem in the world that is easier to debunk than "The Charge of the Light Brigade." We can tear down its rhyme scheme, its structure, its poet, its last verse, its romanticized view of a terrible thing that happened during the Crimean

War, and its entire Victorian view of everything.

We could do that. That's how it's done these days.

But then how would our children grow up to run marathons or climb Mt. Everest or deal with the pain of losing both legs or choose to put others first for no good reason?

It is a poem that is all about honor and that is something the British poets do well. Poetry is the perfect vehicle for teaching honor, if we just let the poetry do its own work in its own time. Entire nations have been born that way. Maybe even most nations.

*Half a league half a league,*
*Half a league onward,*
*All in the valley of Death*
*Rode the six hundred:*

*'Forward, the Light Brigade!*
*Charge for the guns' he said:*
*Into the valley of Death*
*Rode the six hundred.*

*'Forward, the Light Brigade!'*
*Was there a man dismay'd ?*
*Not tho' the soldier knew*
*Some one had blunder'd:*

*Theirs not to make reply,*
*Theirs not to reason why,*
*Theirs but to do & die,*
*Into the valley of Death*
*Rode the six hundred.*

*Cannon to right of them,*
*Cannon to left of them,*
*Cannon in front of them*
*Volley'd & thunder'd;*

*Storm'd at with shot and shell,*
*Boldly they rode and well,*
*Into the jaws of Death,*
*Into the mouth of Hell*
*Rode the six hundred.*

*Flash'd all their sabres bare,*
*Flash'd as they turn'd in air*
*Sabring the gunners there,*
*Charging an army while*
*All the world wonder'd:*

*Plunged in the battery-smoke*
*Right thro' the line they broke;*
*Cossack & Russian*
*Reel'd from the sabre-stroke,*
*Shatter'd & sunder'd.*
*Then they rode back, but not*
*Not the six hundred.*

*Cannon to right of them,*
*Cannon to left of them,*
*Cannon behind them*
*Volley'd and thunder'd;*

*Storm'd at with shot and shell,*
*While horse & hero fell,*
*They that had fought so well*
*Came thro' the jaws of Death,*
*Back from the mouth of Hell,*
*All that was left of them,*
*Left of six hundred.*

*When can their glory fade?*
*O the wild charge they made!*
*All the world wonder'd.*
*Honour the charge they made!*
*Honour the Light Brigade,*
*Noble six hundred!*

My older boys have used their vast store of poetry to get them through some of the toughest training available in the United States military. Once Timothy stood on the deck of the USS Iwo Jima, looking out over the water, and quoted "Crossing the Bar" to quell his own doubts and fears.

*Sunset and evening star,*
  *And one clear call for me!*
*And may there be no moaning of the bar,*
  *When I put out to sea,*

  *But such a tide as moving seems asleep,*
    *Too full for sound and foam,*
  *When that which drew from out the boundless deep*
    *Turns again home.*

  *Twilight and evening bell,*
    *And after that the dark!*
  *And may there be no sadness of farewell,*
    *When I embark;*

  *For tho' from out our bourne of Time and Place*
    *The flood may bear me far,*
  *I hope to see my Pilot face to face*
    *When I have crost the bar.*

As the children matured, or at least as I did, the poems got better. You can never go wrong with Shakespeare, and there did come a day when "The Second Coming" was the perfect poem to memorize.

Just as with our Bible memory and hymns, we always had a new poem to learn and a daily poem to review.

Then I had an idea. In the back of *One-Hundred and One Famous Poems*, there is a supplement of great speeches and documents; so I added a new category to our morning memory. The boys loved memorizing big chunks of Patrick Henry's "Give me Liberty" speech and Timothy would stand on the picnic table in our woods and gloriously proclaim, "Gentleman may cry peace, peace when there is no peace..."

Even the Declaration of Independence reads like a poem, as many of our historical speeches and documents do. After reading it over and over and over again, the words trip over the tongue delightfully, and you find yourself wondering what kind of a man writes like that.

Our memorization work took on new life when we began to have recitation nights with other families. For several years, these were the highlight of our life and helped the children develop deep friendships with other families. We would announce a theme and set a date about six weeks in the future, inviting several families to participate. Our recitation nights grew to be quite large when we were living in the gigantic federal house after the farm. We had a huge covered front porch that was perfect for a stage and, of course, we had food. Whole families were welcome, and even toddlers and adults could take a turn reciting. I think the all-time favorite recitation night was on the theme of Humor. Timothy, Nicholas, and James made up a skit with Christopher as Yoda. My future daughter-in-law, Hannah, and her sister sang "Sisters" from White Christmas, complete with brooms for props. The night Timothy recited *King Henry V's*

St. Crispin's Day speech with the Highland Carol playing in the background was probably one of the most moving moments, while the most incredible feat was when our family friend, fourteen-year-old Colleen Murphy, recited the entire "Pied Piper of Hamlin" poem. It must have taken her half an hour. Then there was the time a couple of brothers rewrote Gilbert and Sullivan's *Modern Major General* into an ode about the dismal failure of modern education. Having an audience brought out the best creative energy in all of us. The children were always eager to recite on those nights, no nagging needed.

We had already successfully been listening to classical music in the mornings and studying composers and artists. In the early years, We would listen to the composer's works in the mornings on cassettes, and then later on CD, and eventually on the computer. Someone would be in charge of getting the music started every morning. Sometimes I would add an excellent biography of a composer, like those by Opal Wheeler, to our read-aloud mix. Low key, yes, but I look back satisfied that while we did not have mega-composer unit studies we did have many years of listening and talking about Handel, Mozart, Bach, Beethoven, Copeland, and many, many others. And we always used the month of December to listen to Handel's "Messiah," using it for our Advent readings, too.

Morning Time allowed us to add things to our days that might not have happened otherwise. Art was one of those things. I would give the children art prints at the beginning of each term and sometimes we would just look at the pictures and talk. Sometimes we would read a biography of the artist like the one my friend Joyce McPherson has written for children about one of our favorite artists, Albrecht Durer.

I used Morning Time to read all sorts of things aloud. We usually had a history stream going and a Christian-living or theology book. Living science books fit, too, and we always, always read a fun novel. If we ended each Morning Time with an entertaining novel we often found ourselves reading 'one more chapter.' Yes, it was a stall tactic by the kids, but it was one I couldn't resist. *Tom Sawyer* is way more fun than math, and I do not regret any of the time we spent reading 'one more chapter.' Later, I will talk more in depth about reading aloud. In Morning Time, the key is not to read any individual book, except the fun book, for too long. Just a tiny bit of each thing, each day.

Morning Time and Charlotte Mason and Classical Education added up to a life built around words and books. I do not believe I became known for this thing called Morning Time because it is anything profound. It is not. Many families have instituted similar things quite organically. What made me different is stubbornness. I just kept at for such a long time that I was able to look back and say, "Yeah, that was worth it. You come, too." A couple of years ago the word 'liturgy' started buzzing around. The minute I heard it I had an epiphany on what it was the made Morning Time work. It is a liturgy. It is a habit that ties the past to the future—a liturgy of love.

Morning Time is a way to collect little grains of sand. It should not be a way to complicate life but rather simplify it. My parents gave me the gift of personal daily Bible reading, the most valuable gift I could have ever received from them. As a mother, you will find me on an occasional Saturday morning studying Matthew Henry or reading Tim

Keller, but my real spiritual reserve comes from a lifetime of daily Bible reading, not complicated Bible study. If you have something that you want your children to assimilate like poetry or scripture or music or Shakespeare, forget the grand schemes, forget what the Konos mom is doing down the street, start giving that thing one or two minutes of your time daily and watch the years roll by.

§

For me, the years did roll by, and they are rolling by for you, too. You are never going to have a lot of time, but you do have a little time here and a little time there, and those little times all add up to a life. Charlotte Mason said that education is an atmosphere, a discipline, and a life. Those words precisely describe Morning Time and why I think it is a perfect way to pull together a Charlotte Mason education.

I had the great privilege of being a part of Ambleside Online from the beginning. Emily and Benjamin were just starting to learn to read, and I put them in year one together. Ambleside gave me the courage to implement a few more things in Morning Time, and it encouraged me to continue with Shakespeare and to add Plutarch.

After my initial success with *A Midsummer Night's Dream*, I grew brave enough to read Shakespeare to the children, just like Susan Schaeffer Macaulay described in *For the Children's Sake*. We would read around three plays a year, one scene a day, year after year. Our habit was to read either Lamb's or Nesbit's retelling, then read the play, then watch a video adaptation of the play. Sometimes each of the children would take a part, but mostly I just read. Often we stopped to figure out what was going on or what something meant. Usually, we slid through mature themes I was not ready to discuss. I fell in love with Shakespeare, the kids not so much, although they did admit knowing Shakespeare's plays came in handy, and there is that Bible verse that says, "Train up a child in the way he should go and, in the end, he will not depart from it." I always tell students they do not have to love Shakespeare. It is understandable. The real sin is assuming that because you do not like his plays there is something lacking in them.

It is probably best to start with the comedies, adding in a couple of tragedies along the way, before moving on to the histories. I like *Much Ado About Nothing* and *The Merchant of Venice* for starters or maybe *The Tempest* and *A Midsummer's Night's Dream*. *The Taming of the Shrew* is also a great one. There are only two plays I don't like: *Pericles* and *Timon of Athens*.

Anne White's study guides on Ambleside Online gave me the confidence to begin reading Plutarch, too. Plutarch tells the story of the Greeks and Romans by comparing a Greek life to a Roman life, making judgements along the way. I had tried to read Plutarch because Charlotte Mason seemed to love him so much, but I would read a sentence and scratch my head. What was he saying? I had no idea. With Anne's help, I decided to try again. It was not love at first sight. I rotated our reading of Shakespeare with our reading of Plutarch. When we finished a play, we started a life.

For years, I alternated Shakespeare and Plutarch covering three lives each year. Then one day I fell in love with Plutarch in much the same way I fell in love with Shakespeare. I started to look forward to reading Plutarch, and when that happened, I started picking up the book even when we were still reading one of Shakespeare's plays. That is how love works. You work hard at it and one day the work becomes joyful. Ordo Amoris. Education is the ordering of our affections. Plutarch is hard to read, but the rewards are there for those willing to try.

Looking back over the years, some of my best memories are of the times when Morning Time got out of control because someone started laughing uncontrollably. At the time it was frustrating but now, looking back, I miss those days. We have at least three real comedians in our family and whenever one of them grew up it left an obvious hole. In the early years, it was usually Nicholas who got us all laughing so hard we couldn't stop. I would be threatening all sorts of dire consequences but doing it through tears of laughter, which made the threats ineffective. When Nicholas first left home we all lived for his phone calls when he would recount hilarious stories of his day.

Years ago, I did an experiment in Morning Time which I blogged about at the time.

> We had a busy day today. At our morning meeting, we went over our school schedule which we start Monday. Whenever we have meetings, it always seems so empty now that Timothy and Nicholas are gone. I was commenting on how this time next year James would not be in our school meetings and I decided to get a visual picture by asking James to leave the room.
>
> I guess you can see where this is going. I then said Nathaniel would not be a part of our school in three years, and he left the room. It made such a striking picture of the future that we kept on

*until Alex and I were left alone in the room. Alex caught on and looked distraught. I wasn't feeling jubilant, myself. Alex perked up when he realized he got to leave the room, too.*

*There I was all by myself in the room. I got up and left, also, leaving the memories of countless morning meetings behind. I do believe I would have made a complete and utter fool of myself if James hadn't resorted to making fun of my little experiment. Tonight while telling Tim of my dismal illustration he reminded me that sometime before Alex left home and I died we would probably have a few grandchildren. That was a real comfort.*

And now we are here. This year would have been the first without Andrew. It would have been the year of just Alex and me. That day, that experiment had planted a seed in my mind that might have saved Alex. It's wrong to hold on to them. The baby, the last baby, gets to grow up, too. I didn't understand when I originally wrote that blog post what it meant that Alex perked up when he got to leave too. I am a mother at heart. I build a home, which seems like a place to stay, but really, it is a place to leave. That is the way of it. Children are meant to grow up. I understand that now. Maybe you have yet to come face-to-face with what that means. I hope you will take courage and allow your children to walk away with grace.

This year Alex went to public school, and it has been good, but nobody can stop me from reading Shakespeare every morning right after my devotions.

# CHAPTER SEVEN

# Exits & Entrances

*"There is not a square inch in the whole domain*
*of our human existence over which Christ,*
*who is Sovereign over all, does not cry, Mine!"*
**Abraham Kuyper**

*D*uring one of our recitation nights, our oldest son graduated from high school. He was eighteen, which meant the other children were now sixteen, fourteen, twelve, eleven, nine, seven, four, and two.

When the nestlings start flying away it happens in reverse order. If you had a baby every eighteen months, your children would leave the nest at approximately the same interval. This usually comes as quite a surprise to mamas who were so busy wiping bottoms they didn't notice that the last diaper had been changed.

One minute you are changing a diaper and the next minute you are rocking your grandbabies. One day you are counting how many children you will have if things go on at this rate and the next minute your youngest is entering high school.

Life may seem to be a litany of the everyday for years on end but it's not. For untold ages, it seemed like I sat on the couch every day listening to someone sound out the letter A. My older boys would walk through the living room and say, "You lead a boring life." It was even more boring when the little child couldn't remember from one second to the next what the letter A said. You know the drill: the rising blood pressure, the trembling book, the absolute disbelief that you feel when he says, "I don't know," not to mention the unendurable phonics lyrics haunting your sleep at night. By the time I taught my youngest to read, I could repeat "a-a-a-a-a-a" endlessly and calmly without losing my temper. That is sanctification. Even though you may have wondered if your children will ever grow up, the day the first one leaves the nest will rock your world. The seismic shift in family life can leave gaping holes. Yet, when the dust settles, something amazing usually takes place. Everyone moves up a notch. Maturity levels rise. Relationships change and blossom. A child who was content to be under the radar is suddenly a leader. I have seen this happen over and over again, but it is always a source of surprise and encouragement to me. Letting a child take the lead is one of the finer arts of motherhood.

One of the more obvious ways to develop this is with a child who has a new learner's permit. Letting a fifteen-year-old chauffeur you around on errands is one of the simplest ways to build a relationship. Just sit quietly in the passenger seat until the child starts talking. Works like a charm. The only bug in the system is that sometimes you have to interrupt the flow of conversation to scream at the child. "Red light, red light!" or "Dog!" This type of yelling will not hurt your relationship. The child just ignores you.

Whenever I went anywhere, especially to baseball games,

I let the little boys carry everything. I am sure some people were appalled to see me walk into a game carrying just my purse while a six year old struggled with a chair or two, but the little boys loved it. After years of this I never had to ask them to carry my bags at the store, they just naturally did it. The point was not to free me up— I am quite capable of carrying my own chair—but to let the young boy know that he is needed and wanted.

The children were now growing up and we were still in New Jersey.

Tim was as southern as a man could be, so living in New Jersey often grated on him. Then, finally, after years of longing for a home down south, we got the word we were moving back. We had hoped to be in Tennessee, but Tim got a job in Alabama, instead.

Tim went on ahead and bought a house for us. The kids and I each picked out what we were looking for in a house. I longed for built-in bookshelves. Tim selected a house in the little town of Elkmont, population 425. It was a beautiful house on three acres, and it was only seventy-five years old. It didn't exactly have built in bookshelves, but bookshelf wallpaper covered the living room. In fact, if you sat in that room and looked through the various open doors you could see six different wallpapers. It would take us years to fix that. The fat baby angels especially fascinated me. Someone went to the store and picked out fat baby angels to put on their walls. The mind boggles. They were the first to go.

We have usually lived out in the country, but this house was right in town. Of course, the town itself was in the country. A friend told me, "They will never accept you here," and much to my southern husband's horror, the first kid we met dubbed us "New Jersey." But we lived on Main Street, so to speak, and the boys played "tennis ball" outside every single day in our field. The whole town drove by daily, always noticing the children.

Tennis ball was a game the boys invented to keep from hitting our neighbors' Corvette with a baseball. It was a competitive game and always went better when my dad was there to umpire. He was not a fair umpire. He umped by attitude, his and theirs. The boys (and Emily) did not discriminate based on age or sex when they played tennis ball. If you were nineteen or four you were expected to pull your weight and then some. Turned out, Emily was quite good at tennis ball, although she refused to play softball.

We joined the Elkmont Youth Baseball league. At first, just a few of the boys played, but we started getting phone calls: "Do you have anyone "this" age? We need an extra player for our team." Before it was over we were doing what we swore never to do, running all over the place to baseball games. Often we did the unthinkable, splitting up the family to make consecutive games. We loved it! Playing sports had been difficult in New Jersey; many teams played on Sunday mornings. In Alabama, not only did they not play on Sundays at all, but they didn't play on Wednesday night, either, because of 'prayer meeting'. This made it much easier on our consciences.

My dad had been teaching the boys baseball for years, and now they had a chance to show their stuff. The first year Christopher played, his coaches kept commenting on how good he was for never having been on a team before. Later, four of them would play some level of college baseball, and James eventually won several NCAA Division III hitting awards and was the Georgia College Baseball Player of the Year.

But our life in Elkmont primarily revolved around when "The Pig" was open. That would be The Piggly Wiggly for y'all Yankees. We were The Pig's main customers. We arrived every morning just as they were opening to get yet another gallon of milk. Some mornings they were waiting for us at the door.

At Christmas, the Elkmont Christmas Parade went right by our house. We sat on our wrap-around southern porch with our neighbors, drinking hot chocolate and watching the parade. Jayber Crow had a barber shop in town, and Barney Fife was our one policeman. He had been told not to give out so many tickets by his superiors, but he still sat on the side road by our house waiting for culprits. The boys got to know him pretty well, which came in handy when they blew things up.

I continued to use Ambleside with the kids while also reading and studying classical education. This combination of Charlotte Mason and classical education never seemed like a problem to me, but often it bothered other people. I started blogging, and my blog was growing. Sometimes people would say, "I thought you said you were classical, but now sound like you are doing a Charlotte Mason education?" and vice versa. This seemed strange to me since a Charlotte Mason education was as rigorous as any classical model I had seen.

When I look back at my time as a blogger, I remember the

first day in New Jersey when we went to the library, and the Internet was on a computer. The boys hovered around while I tried to pry myself off of the thing. I said to them on the way home, "Can you imagine how much time we would waste if we had that in our home?" It is bittersweet now to think of it. I miss those days without a TV or the Internet or cell phones. The Internet has burst educational opportunities wide open, offering many options we never even dreamed of, but not all has been positive. The vast amount of reading my older boys did will never be duplicated by my younger children. All that reading made a difference.

And then there was me and my time. I was often on the Internet while the kids were working on their school lists after Morning Time. It seemed like a blessing, and in many ways it was. I had been at home and isolated for nineteen years, and now I had like-minded friends and mentors at my disposal. Those were heady times. Perhaps I did not watch my children as well as I should have during those years. It seemed like I was always with them, but was I paying attention? It turns out I was not, and some of my children suffered deep wounds because of it. It would be convenient for me to skip this fact, except that I feel compelled to warn other mothers not to make the same mistake.

Blogging helped me take notice of my weakness in the area of grammar. My older boys graduated high school comfortable with writing, but they were weak on mechanics. This weakness wasn't a huge deal, as a semester of college English put most of it to rights. At the same time, comfort and ease in writing can never be gained in a single semester.

As I've indicated previously, Grammar had always been a

problem for me. I wanted the kids to learn more of it than I did but I found they were falling into the same trap as me. They completed grammar workbooks and grammar textbooks, but it never seemed to stick. Finally, I went back to grammar school myself and began taking online grammar courses and reading grammar texts. Often I was still frustrated at my inability to grasp why words did what when. As I learned, I was able to pass along— conversationally— tidbits to the kids, usually when reading their narrations. When I learned "alot" was two words I let everyone know. But I still was not satisfied with how we were learning grammar. I started reading aloud an antique grammar book that my friend Jennifer Frank recommended. Sometimes I didn't even like talking to Jenny because she was such a whiz at the English language, but following my lifelong pattern of hanging out with people who are smarter than me, I tried to learn from Jenny instead of just cringing with embarrassment. I picked up *The Mother Tongue* by Kitteridge and Arnold and began reading tiny sections every morning out loud to the children. We would read and discuss this book for a few minutes each day. A couple of years ago another friend, Amy Edwards, republished *The Mother Tongue* with an answer key. It is an excellent solution to a frustrating problem.

Over the years, my grammar phobia caused me to become addicted to buying grammar resources. I tried to buy my way out of the grammar trap. I owned every grammar diagramming resource ever produced, including pages and pages I printed off the Internet. One day during Morning Time, I picked up a diagramming book and we diagrammed one sentence on the white board. Easy. From there things began to fall into place. Eventually, I bought a Michael Clay Thompson Practice Voyage teacher's book, and we started evaluating sentences according to four different criteria. Still, only one sentence a day. I wish we had done this from the beginning. It takes less than five minutes a day. Suddenly the English sentence began to make beautiful sense. Imagine how many sentences you can evaluate over the long haul?

§

One of the highlights of my life in Elkmont was the day someone from Elkmont Elementary School stopped by on Teacher's Appreciation Day to give me, a homeschool mom, the leftovers of their lunch. Elkmont was the perfect town with the best people on Earth living in it. It was better than Mayberry and Mitford. I thought we would live there forever, but it didn't work out that way.

The kids were growing up. Not only had Timothy left to join the Navy, but he had married an old homeschooling friend, Natalia, and they had one son, Timothy Daniel Rollins III. Nicholas graduated from high school and headed to Florida to the police academy where he spent his first night away from home in a hotel without electricity during a hurricane. Eventually, he married Hannah, a girl he met during our recitation nights in New Jersey. James had also graduated and was looking for a college where he could play baseball. He ended up at Covenant College in Lookout Mountain, Georgia.

Then the company with which Tim had been contracting, offered him a permanent job in Chattanooga, near Lookout

Mountain. Chattanooga was where some of our best friends, the Murphy family, lived. They also had gone crazy and had nine kids. So, after seven years there, we tried to sell our house in Elkmont.

Unfortunately, the recession had hit and there was extreme overbuilding in nearby Huntsville, so no one wanted any acreage (a realtor told us). We could not sell the best home in the world, with the wrap-around porch made for rainy days, and we had to find a rental in Chattanooga. After one long weekend looking we got discouraged. I told the kids it would be a miracle if we did not end up in a horrible house. Then we got our miracle.

Tim found a house being rented by a homeschool family who had moved away. It was only a few years old—a baby house. Our first home in the 'burbs. I loved country living and I adored small-town living, how in the world could I be happy in a neighborhood? The house was pleasant but the yard, as most yards are in Chattanooga, was on a slant. Thankfully, it leaned right down to the woods and while our neighbors on the right and left were pretty close, no house was visible in the back. Mostly, the kids played with the other children in the street. Their shoes started to wear out regularly from the asphalt, but they were having fun. Although it took a while for our kids to lure the neighborhood kids outside, it was nice to see all the kids playing together out doors.

Our house looked small from the outside. The main level was a standard 3 bedroom, 2 bath, but it had a finished basement with another three rooms and a bath. That was where the boys lived. Any amount of boys could go down there, and often I had no idea how many people were down there. Sometimes our family's cars would stretch through the neighborhood, but our neighbors were kind. Now that we were living in the 'burbs, I had to be more proactive about nature study. We could not just walk out the door and be out in the fields with God. But nature is everywhere, and some of the most famous hiking in America is in Chattanooga.

We had always done nature study in Morning Time, but early on I realized that we were not successful at finding something to paint, as Charlotte Mason proposed. We walked often, but dry-brush painting was not my thing. I started giving the boys field guides during Morning Time read-alouds. I would read, and they would draw in their nature notebooks. These artifacts of the past are some of our favorite things to look through. Some of the children were naturally artistic and some not so much, but all drew in their nature notebooks most mornings. James was not so artistic, and he became famous for his daily drawing of a snake wrapped around a pole.

For years, our children had daily lists which they marked off. They mostly did the same things each day. I never successfully found another way to school. Their days looked something like this: math, Morning Time, Latin with me or other teacher-intensive subjects, any language arts work like handwriting or spelling drills on the computer, written narration, and reading for at least two hours. Their reading lists covered almost all things we might call 'subjects'. For years, I made out weekly lists, rotating in the books I wanted them to read, but I drooled over programs like Sonlight where it was all laid out for mom. Every year I would total up how much it would cost to buy a complete year of a pre-planned curriculum for each of the children. It totaled exactly one arm and one leg, and my husband was convinced we needed both.

My most popular blog post ever was about this dilemma:

*It's that time of year when all the glossy homeschool catalogs begin to pour into the mailbox. First I feel hopeful. ("Next year is gonna be great.") Then I feel overwhelmed. ("Can I fit in a complete year of Sonlight and Memoria Press online courses at the same time for the same child?") Then I feel inadequate. ("Why are my kids so ordinary when I am trying so hard?") Then I feel angry at my husband. ("Seriously, man, work some overtime.") Within a few days I feel like a total homeschool failure. ("I can't even afford to put them all in public school.") It would be less sinful for me to peruse the Sport's Illustrated swimsuit issue. At least I couldn't even pretend I could look like those models. This year it has been a little bit worse for me. I started to notice that all the catalogs had testimonies of how God provided that curriculum to the family and how it had saved the mother's sanity and how, without that curriculum, the kids would just be ordinary, but God had given the family an answer to their prayers through great products and online teachers who knew things no mother could teach. In some cases that answer to prayer was costing the family close to $10,000 a year, and here I was agonizing over buying one math program. It almost tempted me to think, "maybe God doesn't love me since he doesn't seem to care about my sanity at all."*

*But it doesn't stop there. Some catalogs mention how important is for us not to skimp on quality, to spend our money providing great opportunities for our children. And there seems to be a huge number of one-income, large, homeschooling families who can afford to have their priorities straight while my priorities are skewed towards food and clothing. Now let me just say right here, if you can afford to take advantage of the myriads of homeschool opportunities that cost an arm and a leg, then more power to you. I don't have a beef with your beautiful family, your money, or your priorities. I am not even talking to you right now at all. You may leave the room. If you publish beautiful catalogs full of testimonies of how God used your product to save crazy moms, preach on. You landed a big endorsement. Use it. I believe in the free market of commerce. You don't need to waste your time getting mad at me, with God driving all that business your way. I hope you don't mind, then, if I engage in the free market of ideas. I would like to turn away now from the beautiful families and the beautiful publishers and talk to the rest of us. It's going to be all right. Sing this little song: 'give it your best and pray that it's blessed and He'll take care of the rest . . .'*

I have been doing this spring dance for over twenty years. For over twenty years I have tallied up my dream homeschool and then had to ditch the whole thing as reality set in. Some years I have spent virtually zero dollars. Some years I have had to sell things I needed in order to stay above water. I have been content and I have been bitter. Some days I am pretty sure I messed up the whole lot of 'em, and some days I can't stop bragging about the people they have become. Teachers are wonderful and money *is wonderful and opportunities are wonderful, but none of those things are the definition of education. Education is an atmosphere, a discipline, and a life. A catalog can't provide any of those things, but you can. You can make your home the kind of atmosphere that encourages learning. You can teach your children and require your children to have the discipline they need to learn hard things. You can remember that you and your children will be learning for the rest of your lives. It doesn't all hinge on next year or the next day's mail. If the catalogs are making you crazy, throw them away. Read Charlotte Mason's six volume series instead. I am.*

§

One summer, after I was down to four students at home, I decided to see if I could plan out one hundred and eighty days before the year started for each child. I spent about a month in the summer doing this, and it was fun. Somehow, some way what I planned worked. The next year, though, I was thinking more and more of nature study because Chattanooga is considered one of the greatest outdoor cities in the country, and we were not taking advantage of that. I decided only to plan one hundred and forty-four days leaving one day a week open for hiking. I still planned almost the same amount of school work, but I divided it up over a fewer number of days. Honestly, planning one hundred and forty-four days made my plan more realistic. That year we didn't hike every week, but we got in far more hikes than ever before. As I get older, I am seeing that Charlotte Mason's ideas are not just for children. Turns out moms are born persons, too. I can still make hiking a priority in my own life, and there are always the grandchildren. I make it a point to take them on little hikes every time I see them.

During these years, Emily was growing up. I had been through puberty with six boys so far, and I was terrified of what it would be like with a girl. I knew my own mother had put 'the curse' on me after my own disastrous pubescent years where I stormed around telling her I hated her almost daily. But Emily seemed to manage it much more gracefully than me. The first blip came about over her clothing.

Emily has an artistic spirit and her clothes started to reflect that. The only problem came when she wanted to wear shorter skirts with heels to church. Emily and I have different memories of this time. She absorbed a legalistic message about women's and girls' attire. I thought we were at least trying to communicate grace and wisdom. That is one of the great mysteries of family communication. People perceive things differently. But I did learn a few things along the way. It always seemed to Emily that the burden of modesty fell on the girl and that Christians taught that women were responsible for men's lustful thoughts. This just didn't seem right to her. It let men and boys off the hook for their own struggles by blaming lust on women. Eventually, I learned to tell my boys that there was no sense worrying about the fact that immodesty was everywhere; they had to wrestle with their own hearts on this issue.

Looking back, it is easy to see that it was hard on a girl to be around so many boys all the time, none of whom related to her emotionally. She learned to hide her feelings, and that was harmful. By the time I caught a hint that Emily was isolated emotionally there were not that many other options for her. We had moved from Alabama to Tennessee during critical years in her life, leaving behind her support system of friends. I longed for Emily to have a sister and often wondered why God had not given her one, until I looked up one day and realized that Emily did have sisters. She had three sisters-in-law, Natalia, Hannah, and Vanessa. Suddenly, her life was filled with the thing I longed for her.

If you met Emily today, you would see a vibrant, spiritual, lovely woman. She is strikingly beautiful and people often commented, "no wonder she has so many brothers." My husband always wanted the boys to treat her like a princess, but that didn't really happen as much as it should have. Now she has a wonderful Christian husband, Anibal, who does.

One reason I haven't written about her as much as the boys is that she is just one. If there were two girls I could share more and keep their identities private. I can tell boy stories all day long without stepping over privacy boundaries; it is easy to hide in a group. But Emily is a quiet, private girl, and I respect that. I tried to take her with me wherever I went, and I do have a personal opinion, gleaned from Dr. James Dobson, that boys in puberty should never babysit. It was wonderful for me to have a daughter, to go shopping with, to update my wardrobe, to talk about feminine things. When Emily left home, I deeply missed those things. She single-handedly helped me morph from jumpers and Keds to jeans and boots.

Her wardrobe updates were not always successful, of course. Sometimes I didn't look trendy, I just looked silly. I had to dress my age not hers. But I will always joyfully remember her help. When she moved out, it took me a while to learn how to buy clothes without her advice.

After living in the same house in Chattanooga for six years, the day came when our landlord had to sell it. Because it lacked a real yard, we were hesitant to buy it for our coming older years. We had moved into that house with seven children still in and out of the home, and some at college. Nathaniel married Vanessa while we lived there and Emily married Anibal. We left with only two children still at home.

The move was traumatic. We were truly downsizing. I had to get rid of a lifetime of possessions, including school records and books, to fit into the new rental. Right in the middle of the move, Andrew came down with mononucleosis and ended up in the hospital. That left Alex and me to bear the main brunt of the packing. This was drastically different than our many earlier moves when we had muscle to spare. It was Christmas time, too. So we did the unthinkable and bought a fake tree to put up at the old house while we were moving. We thought we would buy our real tree when we got moved into the new house, but we were so exhausted we ended up transporting the artificial tree intact to the new house. For the first time in thirty-five years, we had an artificial tree. Life is hard. We disappoint ourselves. We liked this new house all right. We didn't love it, but it did have a flat yard to play croquet in—my favorite game!

We moved into the rental on December 15. Sometime in June, Tim called a realtor friend to see if maybe in the next five years we would qualify again for a loan to buy a house. The realtor said, "You qualify now." And so we started looking at houses. On September 1st we closed on The Tree

House, a glorious little house, although smaller than the last one. It is a good thing we had started downsizing.

When I talk about downsizing, it means one thing: I got rid of books. I am not sure how many books I had at the peak. I have always felt that numbering your books is as prideful as David numbering the people in the book of Chronicles. We had library shelves in our dining room covering all the walls. We had bookshelves purchased from old libraries in the den and every other room in the house except the bathrooms. When we left Alabama, I got rid of many books, sending the mediocre ones to Goodwill and the best ones to the grand-children, selling others, but I still had a lot of books left. I got rid of more when we moved to the smaller rental, and I sold much of my homeschooling stuff as the younger boys grew out of it. It turns out I never really needed every single Latin program ever written. I made the final cull when we moved to The Tree House, getting rid of the bulk of my homeschool curricula. The curricula was not so important, after all. It was always the books. Moms always ask, "What exactly is a living book?" Now I know. It is what I still have on my shelves.

# CHAPTER EIGHT

# What Are Little Boys Made of?

*"We make men without chests and expect from them virtue and enterprise. We laugh at honor and are shocked to find traitors in our midst."*

**C.S. Lewis**

I wanted my first baby to be a girl. Boys were alien creatures to me. I probably knew less about boys than many people and more than some. I had spent my childhood in the gym where my dad had his office and at the baseball field. At least, I knew what they smelled like. But like most young women, I wanted something more resembling myself for my first baby. I knew the odds were against me. Boys overran my husband's family. He had one sister and four brothers. His Dad came from a family of nine boys and one girl aptly called "Sister." We had more nephews than nieces. I knew what I was getting into, but I still wanted a girl. I wanted a girl right up until the moment I looked Timothy in the eyes; then I wanted a boy.

After that, I didn't care so much. A second boy could play with the first. A third boy would be easier. A fourth boy would save money. A fifth boy would save energy on my part. A sixth boy only made sense. A seventh son seemed like a necessity; I would surely ruin a girl. But the seventh boy would have to wait. As you already know, we had a girl, followed by Andrew and Alex. Eight boys, one girl.

For years, people thought Tim and I were trying for a girl, and truthfully, it got pretty annoying when they constantly asked me, "Are you hoping for a girl?" Some even said, "We are praying you have a girl." I tried, sometimes successfully, not to say, "It is too late. It is already a boy or a girl." After the first baby I never really cared whether we had a boy or a girl. The determination of its sex was already a given. What did it matter what I thought?

The boys ended up doing plenty of crazy things. Some I knew about, some I heard about, and some I will never know, thankfully.

Most of their early adventures were my fault. I tried hard to be an understanding mother. I tried not to hover. But sometimes this tactic had unintended consequences.

When Timothy was five, I let him go out in the woods behind our house during Nicholas's nap. No big deal. We were reading aloud *Little House in the Big Woods*, so it seemed the obvious thing to let him do. He was gone for quite a while. When Nicholas woke he went outside and heard yelling. Timothy was screaming from the woods. I was about seven months pregnant at the time, so I waddled as fast as I could into the woods towards the little yelling voice. In the distance, I could see Timothy. He was sinking in a swamp. I didn't even know there was a swamp out there. He had sunk to his thighs and had been yelling for a long time. It was January in New Jersey, and he was sinking in freezing water. I could not walk across the swamp because I was far too heavy. Finally, I asked, "Are you wearing boots? Slip out of the boots and see if that works." Poor little guy, he cried back to me so sorrowfully, "They're Papa's boots. I cannot leave them in the mud." Glorious day. Thank goodness he was wearing huge boots. I told him to slip out of them and see if he could make it to me. He left the boots in the mud, where they are to this day, and slithered across the swamp to me. I quickly got him home and into a warm bath with a mug of hot chocolate. What a silly woman I was, letting my five-year-old explore alone, but Timothy was always like that, ready to assume he could do anything and I was like that too, always ready to believe him.

Around that same time, he came to me and said he was going to go to a baseball game. I winked and said, "sure go ahead," confident that we understood each other. What I didn't understand was that the boys had seen field lights in the distance. They thought we lived near a ball field, but we did not.

After a little while, I went to "watch" the ballgame with them. I could not find them. My five year-old and my three year-old and Weatherby, our dog, were gone. Once again I ran around searching for them. First I ran to our pond where I was sure I would find them drowned. Then, not finding them there, I ran to the road where far, far away I saw Weatherby trotting towards me. Behind him were two little specks walking home.

I ran to them as fast as I could, full of rebukes. They were stunned. Hadn't I said they could go to a ballgame? They had walked almost a mile down the road before they had crossed a bridge over a creek. That reminded them of all my dire warnings about water, so they turned around. Once again, I had let my desire not to hover cause me to make a mistake. I am a true believer in guardian angels.

Soon after that, we had our first fire. An upstairs mattress caught fire. The fire department came, and so did a few of our friends who had monitoring radios. That was embarrassing. We didn't find out who set the fire until months later, maybe years, but our efforts to find out go down in history as one of the worst parenting mistakes ever. Let's just say we got a confession but it turned out to be the wrong one. I would love a do-over on that episode.

Many years later while living in the federal mansion after the farm, one of the boys took the ashes from the fireplace and dumped them in the woods on some pine needles during a drought. We looked out back to see our woods on fire. We all ran out with hoses and pots and pans and stamped and stamped until the fire department came. They were condescendingly nice.

A week later they were even nicer when one early morning a man came tearing up our long driveway in a car yelling "Your house is on fire!" The chimney had caught on fire and flames were stretching out of the third floor. The fire chief just laughed. After all, this one was not actually our fault. Thankfully, the flames were quickly put out. I have had to use the word "thankfully" a lot in this chapter. I will have to use it quite a bit more.

Once, after driving into Athens, a nearby city, to run some errands, I came back into town to pay our water bill at the little city hall. The clerk looked at my name and then up at me and said, "I think there was an explosion at your house."

I looked at her calmly and said, "Probably."

She proceeded to explain that Barney Fife had checked it out, and all was well. One son had filled a metal barrel with as many leaves as he could squeeze in and then filled it with gasoline to burn the leaves. Apparently leaves give off nitrogen, and nitrogen goes boom! The boom was so loud it shook the town. We lost an old apple tree that day, and some eyebrows.

A few years later, I got to experience the nitrogen boom again. Timothy was returning from special forces training, and his adrenaline was wacky when he first got home. Instead of coming in the front door and hugging his awaiting family like in a Norman Rockwell painting, he decided to climb the roof, come in an upstairs window, and surprise us by coming down the stairs rather than through the front door. I wasn't too surprised. I had learned to be impervious, but the little people were thrilled.

A couple of days later one of the boys went out to burn some leaves that had been falling from the gorgeous maple trees in our yard. Timothy was inside full of adrenaline. Boom!! The house shook. Timothy grabbed me and threw me under the table, thinking we were under attack. I have never figured out who he thought was attacking us. I scrambled out from under the table as quickly as I could, assuming our son had blown himself up and maybe others. He was fine. He had the foresight to make a fuse before lighting the huge pile of leaves and the sense to make his little brothers back up. But Barney dropped by again.

Once, while I was visiting my parents, I received this

phone call from one of the boys: "Mama, I blew up the computer." He had blown it up by trying to hardwire the computer to the electrical outlet. He was working for a wiring guy at the time and thought he would see about hooking our computers to a homemade network. The electricity fried the computer and the outlet. He was alive; I was umoved.

§

One of our sons won the nickname "human tornado."

In Alabama, we frequently had tornado warnings and even tornados. Once we lost a tree in our backyard to straight-line winds and whole swaths of our neighborhood were hit. The first day we lived there we had to go into what became known as the Hobbit Hole, a cement block square covered with a mound of dirt near the side of the house. It was super weird and cute at the same time but no fun to hang out in with eleven people. We did not go in there when the weatherman said "Head to a shelter." We waited until we heard the roar.

This particular boy did not have a driver's license when one day he decided, on his own, to move the truck. He got 'reverse' and 'drive' mixed up and plowed into the garage, creating a gaping hole in the side of it. Our neighbors kept asking if the tornado had hit the house. We told them it was "the human tornado."

My husband's field of work is mostly concerned with safety issues. He tried to bring this expertise to our home. At one point, he carefully illustrated to the boys the idea of high risk behavior using a basket of eggs. "High-risk" became a key word he used when communicating to the boys. But rather than learning it was something to avoid, it almost seemed like they took on the idea as a goal. One day we found three year old Benjamin jumping up and down on top of the washing machine singing, "High risky, high risky, I am playing high risky."

Before Emily was born, the boys had no clue about the female sex. When little girls came over and wanted to play various games that the boys were playing, the boys always thought it was odd. I would try to explain, but they just thought girls were a foreign species.

One day, James asked me a question that started with, "Mama, when you were a little boy did . . . ?"

I replied, "I wasn't ever a little boy, James, I was a little girl."

He gasped deeply and cried out "Uh-Uh!"

I could tell it was a revelation for him, and not a good one. The boys needed a sister.

§

Of course, having all those boys meant I was constantly trying to clean the house. How many women can look up at a twelve foot ceiling and see footprints? How does one get bare feet prints on a ceiling that high? We will never know. I had to make a rule, "No walking on the ceiling."

I learned early on that the boys would embarrass me, sometimes on purpose, sometimes accidentally. Once when Tim was out of town, I got called into our pastor's office to discuss James. When I got there, several families were there. It turns out James had been listening to country music. In that church, at that time, that was shocking. I was completely confused. I turned to one other boy in the room and said, "Don't you listen to rock music sometimes?" not thinking this was a big deal. The whole room erupted, and the meeting was suspended because none of the parents knew their children were listening to music of which they disapproved.

The Bible talks of some people's sins going before them and some following behind. In our family, they go before us.

When I first read Paul Tripp's *Age of Opportunity*, I thought his teenagers sounded dreadful. Oh, how naive I was. I was shocked that he seemed to take their dangerous driving in stride. My boys would never be bad drivers, I was convinced of it. For the sake of this book, however, I decided to count all the car wrecks I can remember. I can think of seven right off the bat. Thankfully, none of them were serious. Oh, we lost a few of those cars, but no serious injury ever occurred. Not even when the little Honda was flipped upside down in a ditch after one son lost control going over a railroad track. We pulled that Honda, with over 300,000 miles out of the ditch and it chugged itself home, making us lifelong fans of Honda. James called once because his car was on fire. There was no driving home in that burnt wreck.

I am not really so impervious as I like to pretend. Deep down inside, I think every late night call is bad news. I am always mentally prepared to hear the boys have hurt themselves. Often, when I hear a siren, I mentally note where each of my children are and call the ones I am unsure of. Most of my children have gotten shaken calls from me asking them if they are all right. Even yesterday, when Andrew went to workout, and an ambulance whizzed into our neighborhood, I kept thinking, "Where did Andrew say he would be working out?"

Still, I do not stay up late waiting for the children to come in at night like I did in the early years; sleep is too important. I just ask that Andrew text when he comes in so when I wake up in the middle of the night I won't have to go outside to see if his car is there. Many a night I have walked outside in my bare feet and pajamas to make sure everyone was in.

It turns out that the cry of my heart is still the same every single day and night. Are all the children in? I truly have no greater joy than to hear that my children walk in the truth. It is my main joy in life apart from the joy of knowing Jesus loves me. I wasn't always the best mother. I was certainly trying to be, but looking back now, I am sad I let my little 5-year-old walk alone in the woods. I am sad that I abused my power to wrench a confession from an innocent child. I am sad that I spent time on the computer when I should have been paying attention to my children.

I would be even sadder than I could bear for these lapses (and worse ones) if it wasn't for Jesus. He bore my sins in his body on the cross that I might die to sin and live to righteousness.

§

I almost titled this chapter "Boys Will Be Boys."

Over the years, that is one of the central questions mothers have asked me. "Is this the way boys act?" Often this question comes about in reference to some sort of bullying.

Bullying is not manly behavior, and it is something we need to be looking for diligently. It takes some practice to tell the difference between boyish fighting and bullying. We had plenty of fights in our home, some wrestling, and even some fisticuffs. It is hard to imagine that much testosterone in one home. As a woman, I was always baffled by it and didn't ever really understand it, but the only real lasting damage came when someone got away with bullying others.

We are living in an increasingly feminized society. Some people view that as an increasingly civilized society, but it has left our boys with deep desires for honor but few outlets for displaying it appropriately.

I often think it was hard for my boys to read all those old books where the bully got thrashed when in our culture thrashing is something shameful. How do you stand up for a maiden in distress in a culture where the maiden carries her own weapon? I am not saying women should not be strong; I am just pondering the ways our new cultural norms leave boys drifting.

Think about some favorite family read-aloud. Pick any random book from the past and try to imagine your son truly behaving like the hero in the book behaved but in our culture instead. It most likely would be considered shameful behavior now. Certainly, modernity tries to offer protection to victims, and that is good. Men cannot be bullies in this brave new world, and that is right. But that still leaves us with a state of affairs highly skewed toward feminine values. These are just things to think about; I do not have all the answers. In fact, I don't have any answers, but I know that we need to face up to the problem that there is less and less room in our culture for men with chests, and when men don't have chests they often victimize women rather than protect them.

During puberty, boys need strong male role models and accountability. A mother cannot provide this, and this is one reason I am less fond of homeschooling boys through high school than I used to be. At least, I am not fond of mom being the sole teacher. I see now I was in way over my head in things pertaining to sex, pornography, and hormones. Do not feel distressed if you find you need professional help in these difficult areas. I wish I had sought more help.

It is hard to explain puberty to young parents. I was not too worried about it in the early years. I arrogantly felt that our homeschool lifestyle would protect us from the dangers other families were facing. On some level that was true, but there was more to puberty than just what appeared on the surface. When my first son reached adolescence I was confident; knowing my last son is heading that way, I am much less so. One reason I tremble so much more is that I have been dealing with this for twenty years now. When my daughter mentioned that to me one day, it was almost a relief. No wonder we had been through some tough years.

I found there are two tiers to puberty. Just when you get through one tier and you breathe a sigh of relief, the next, more intense tier starts. The first level is usually the basic moodiness of the blossoming teen. It helps just to laugh your way through that level. The next is much more complicated because, for boys, it is a time of becoming men, and that often means challenging authority in an effort to be an authority.

In our home, the desire to be the alpha dog in a kennel of alpha dogs created much discord.

Being a female in a mostly male house was often confusing.

Emily recently told me a story which left me laughing while also feeling a little sad.

Each morning I used Morning Meeting as a place to remind the children of hygienic or necessary life skills. Obviously, lifting the toilet seat was an important life skill and one to which the boys did not often adhere. One of the boys even made a habit of trying to hit the toilet from outside the bathroom door because he didn't like to walk on the bathroom floor. Talk about a circle of logic! So I harped. I nagged. And no one listened. No one, that is, except my earnest little daughter who thought for years she had to lift the toilet seat.

When the boys are home and telling stories to each other, I am always amazed at the things I knew nothing about (and often wish I still didn't know about). I thought I was with them all the time. Yet they managed to do so many things when I wasn't paying attention.

§

Last night I was talking to Timothy on the phone, and he said that he had been making up stories to tell his own children every night before they went to bed, and lately he was telling about his real adventures as a boy. I didn't know the half of it, but I do remember when he was five he prayed for a pocket knife and finished his prayer, "and please, God, when you give me the knife could you also provide a small animal for me to kill." God answered that prayer with the knife and mice, snapping turtles, eels, snakes, etc.

When it came to physical confrontations, I had a rule: No physical touching. The boys knew if they were going to fight it better not be in front of me. They were not scared of me at all; they just knew how to play the system.

Most families don't have eight sons, but most moms are pretty naive about the sons they do have, just as I was. I read once that a nine-year-old boy is the most pleasant of all children to be around. I believe that is true. As moms, we have this baby, and then we have this nine-year-old boy, and our relationship with him is sweet to us, but that is not the end of the story.

Boys must grow up and be men, and that is a difficult transition made more difficult by the fact that it is a mostly private change. We don't always see the changes taking place, and we imagine that all is the same as it has been until one day that sweet little fellow is moody or angry or short with us. What have we done to deserve that? His voice squeaks and then rumbles. We hadn't noticed, but he is suddenly not that wonderfully sweet nine-year-old. He wants to be a man. If there is one thing a boy turning into a man does not want, it is to be confronted with his mother's hand-wringing and whining. It is time to step away from the boy and let him become a man; this is probably the hardest lesson of mothering.

Good mothering is not smothering; we all know that, but somehow it is much harder not to smother than it seems. The anxiety of a worried mother does not instill the boy/man with confidence. The truth is, women are often afraid of masculinity. It is not our thing. Like Aslan, it is not safe.

Ultimately, we have to let our boys be men. Whatever satisfaction we got out of our relationship with our son must be turned toward the one who is better than ten sons. Isn't that how our hearts work? Our longings are triggers which find their fulfillment in Christ. That fulfillment is always available to you as a mother even in the midst of letting go of relationships we treasure.

I can promise you that Christ is big enough to fill the void, and after you learn to trust him, your son will learn to trust that you will not let your femininity get in the way of his manhood.

CHAPTER NINE

# *Cottleston Pie*

*"The Aconleighs were obliged to face the fact,*
*as parents must sooner or later, that their*
*children had broken loose from control*
*and had taken charge of their own lives."*
**Nancy Mitford, *The Pursuit of Love***

*T*he Tree House, our first house with a name, and where we live as I write, is on almost three wooded acres in a neighborhood with a community pool. We have neighbors, but they are not too close. Deer, turkey, and other critters fill our backyard. We have a wrap-around back deck and a screened-in porch. The glass windows and doors along our back wall are always open. We made the offer a few minutes after seeing the house. It is everything I wanted. I walk about in a daze. I am exhausted from moving twice in one year, but I am astounded by where I find myself every morning.

It is as if, out of the blue, God picked us up and plopped us down in this beautiful place. It is truly our dream house. Tim and I hope we grow old here or, at least, we hope it is our last move. I have already had the joy of taking two sets of grandchildren for nature walks on the property and, last week, while hiking with Anabella and Savanna, a deer bounded right in front of us. Their little hearts were beating with joy and excitement — and so was mine.

We have not had the pleasure of living in one place all our lives like my old Mennonite friend Rhoda Hostetter. This last place, Chattanooga, has been voted the best town in America by Outdoor Magazine. I guess they didn't know about Elkmont. But honestly, Chattanooga has turned out to be a most excellent place. Every morning I revel in its beauty. The mountains loom up majestically. I look to the hills from whence cometh my help. This morning, as I drove to the valley from our ridge, I could see the fog hovering over the waters of the Tennessee River below, and it felt like I was in Heaven.

§

For these many years of wandering, Tim and I have often read Psalm 107 with longing. Way back in Massachusetts we heard a sermon on it that we never forgot. The guest pastor who gave it spent the afternoon with us. He was a modest man in his own eyes. He felt discouraged about the sermon, but we never forgot it. We were wanderers looking for a home, a place. What we could not do for ourselves, God has done.

> *Let the redeemed of the Lord tell their story—*
>     *those he redeemed from the hand of the foe,*
> *those he gathered from the lands,*
>     *from east and west, from north and south.*
> *Some wandered in desert wastelands,*
>     *finding no way to a city where they could settle.*

*They were hungry and thirsty,*
*  and their lives ebbed away.*
*Then they cried out to the Lord in their trouble,*
*  and he delivered them from their distress.*
*He led them by a straight way*
*  to a city where they could settle.*
*Let them give thanks to the Lord for his unfailing love*
*  and his wonderful deeds for mankind,*
*for he satisfies the thirsty*
*  and fills the hungry with good things.*

Our marriage has lasted thirty-six years so far. World Magazine once ran an article that interviewed couples married for over fifty years. All of the couples said there were times when they could have easily separated or divorced. They had many legitimate gripes with one another and many ups and downs in their marriages, but somehow they had stayed together. Not one of the couples regretted it. They all spoke glowingly of each other and their joy in making it work for the long haul. Their companionship and shared heritage and deep love were worth fighting for.

Our years on the farm stretched us to our limits, leaving our marriage fragile. We all have faults. Some periods of life bring those faults to the forefront, making it seem that we are only our faults. When we moved to the farm, we were full of hopes and dreams. As those dreams faded with the overwhelming reality of our daily life, the crushing financial burdens of the ancient farmhouse, the vast acreage needing attendance, my physical weakness as pregnancy after pregnancy took its toll, and the sheer knowledge that we were not making this farm a better place, our marriage was stretched past the human breaking point.

Later, when we lost one of our homes, we suffered another round of shame and blame. If we had not been Christians committed to the ideal of marriage, we would not have stayed married under those bleak realities. It also helped that we could not afford to separate. Our human failings had harmed our marriage, but our heavenly Father did not leave it at that. Tim and I both steeled ourselves to stick it out and, in the end, we are both thankful that God gave us that gift. We have seen just how God works in lives, changing each of us as individuals and healing our marriage in ways we assumed were impossible.

Truly with God, all things are possible, even good marriages.

Tim Keller has said that marriage is just two people good at forgiveness. When we were young and in love, forgiveness didn't seem so important. We did not think we could sin against each other. Oh, sure, we knew the minor disappointments of finding the toothpaste lid off, but the shock of young love is discovering how hard the work of forgiveness is.

Nothing in this world is harder than forgiveness. It is God's ultimate gift to us, and it is ours to give to one another. It costs us dearly on the front end. It costs us our pride and sometimes our own self-hood, but once given it does more good for the forgiver than the forgiven. Of course, marriage is difficult for all of us, but in almost every case (there are exceptions) it is worth fighting for. I married at eighteen and have weathered some pretty rough patches along the way, but to this day, I do not regret that decision. Marriage is good. It is good for us. It is good for our children. It is good for the church. And it is good for the culture.

One of the primary causes of tension in our marriage came from, simply put, bad teaching of Christian principles of submission. During the 1980s and '90s, Christian men were encouraged to be the 'head of their homes.' The Christian woman was taught to be submissive in all things. I believe this was a great disservice to Christian manhood. It became a sort of enabling. Instead of the Christian man growing and improving as a person, he often became trapped in his own headship. His wife was no longer a 'help' to him because she was essentially an enabler or 'yes-man.' How sad.

Many excellent men, like my husband, Tim, became stuck in bad patterns of behavior which left them floundering in weakening relationships. When I read Henry Cloud and John Townsend's *Boundaries in Marriage* I realized that my outward compliance of submission without question was harming my husband. I began to move awkwardly toward more honesty in my relationship with my husband and he began to respond positively.

Submission was never meant to enable weakness. Both my husband and I had misunderstood true submission. I am happy to say that this enlightenment brought about great growth in our relationship. I felt sad that I had not been honest with him sooner.

§

I have also had to transition from being a middle-aged mom to an older mom. I started noticing, recently, that I am the same age as many of the grandparents at Alex's baseball games.

What is it like to be an older mom?

For the longest time, I was a young mother, and it seemed like I would be one forever. Perhaps if we hadn't moved, I would still think of myself that way. But in moving, I was forced to see myself in a new light, and it has been an adjustment. Also, my face is sagging in the mirror. Last Sunday I went to church, and because my husband works two Sundays a month I sat in my pew with just two boys: Andrew and Alex. I am sure to many people I looked like a divorcee struggling to church with her children. It was a bit of a shock for me to watch my family dwindle over the last ten years, because ten short years ago we had all of our children squished into the pew with us. And while my other children are all generally in a pew somewhere, they are not with me. And since we recently moved, no one here knows that a couple of years ago I needed the longest pew in the church, while now I am virtually invisible. There is just no way to see something like that coming, and maybe it is wrong of me to even mention it to young mothers.

But it is much harder for me to break into new social groups without young children and I am even older than the parents of the teens at church. And here is another problem I have. When I was younger if I talked to young mothers we shared experiences. Now, if I share an experience with a young mother, it seems like I am a know-it-all and young mothers don't want to hear any advice. I understand that. I was like that too. I was confident. But it would be nice to be able to share my experiences now, mother-to-mother, without feeling like  I am interfering. What I am really doing is commiserating.

Of course, I don't know that young mothers resent my re-membrances. I just feel that maybe they might, and that is why I try not to say anything to them—except to my daugh-ters-in-law who know enough of my failures to know I am certainly not a know-it-all. I did rack up quite a few stories over the years. It is strange, but for years and years I just forgot everything, and then when my grandchildren were born I started to remember what it was like to be a young mom. And I remembered how cute the little boys were and how much fun we had and how old ladies always asked me why the baby didn't have a hat on and how I resented that. I would never tell a young mother to put a hat on her baby, but I would like to tell the story of how I didn't put a hat on my baby and how all the little old ladies gasped. You see, those old ladies had lived in a world before central everything and they had often walked to church. How could they imagine that something so vital to survival in their time was now un-necessary? That's why they were the old ladies, and I was the young mother.

And that is how it goes. Young mothers grow old, and the world changes, and they never see it coming. No matter how many times someone tells you, "this too shall pass," it always seems to be trite.

In spite of all of this whining, I don't mind growing old. I breathe a sigh of relief when I hear a young mother say she didn't get any sleep because her babies were sick. I like to sleep, and if it weren't for hormones, I would get some. It is hard work having young children, utterly exhausting, and truly only for the young. A couple of hours with my grand-children and I am whooped; happy, but whooped.

My mother-in-law, who had six children used to say to me, "I don't know how you do it," and I would think, "What do you mean? You did it, too."

But now I understand.

When I look at young mothers, I, too, don't know how they do it. But watching the four little boys in the pew in front of me doesn't make me feel like a know-it-all: it reminds me of four other little boys once upon a time, and that makes me happy.

CHAPTER TEN

# Further Up &
# Further In

*"Education eventually comes down to a conversation
between a young person and an old person."*
**Wendell Berry,**
**2012 Paideia Prize Acceptance Speech**

To gain some control over my life, I turned to educational philosophy. This annoyed my children. I could never just watch a movie. I had to think about it out loud. Alex likes to tease me about my "fun facts," but I have noticed recently that he has a few of his own.

The 'ages and stages' model of classical education had left me hopelessly confused. With so many ages and stages in my family, how could I ever figure out when to chant the Greek alphabet and with whom and when to dissect a syllogism?

I had, of course, followed Charlotte Mason's philosophy for years, but I was always second guessing myself. Truthfully, almost all the methods I tried ended up coming from a similar philosophy. It is no surprise that almost all of the classical vendors started out as Charlotte Mason enthusiasts.

Besides the obvious classical and Charlotte Mason worlds,

I was pulled towards other methods, also.

The Robinson Method was created by a dad who had lost his wife to cancer but wanted to keep homeschooling while working his full time job as a scientist. So he developed a method in which his children studied math for two hours a day, wrote a narration, and read for two to three hours a day. This was not that different from Charlotte's philosophy, and it was a lifesaver for me during the most intense years when I was homeschooling seven children while keeping up with toddlers, too.

I was also drawn to the Principle Approach with its deep philosophical underpinnings and orderly materials. I spent loads of money buying all the books but just couldn't make it work in our family. It was after the failure of this massive endeavor that I turned to workbooks.

All the while, classical education was becoming popular. Our church even began a classical school. I read everything I could about it, including Dorothy Sayer's famous essay. I bought catalogs from classical vendors and, quite frankly, lusted over their products. I added Latin to our days, first trying one program and then another and then another until I finally settled on studying Wheelock's Latin on my own. Then we at least got through *Latin For Children*, Level 1, without a hitch. I struggled so hard to teach Latin, I never got around to teaching Logic. In the back of my mind this was not a big deal. The boys were already backing me into a corner logically and I was not sure I wanted to empower them with Logic. I had learned the best way to fight their logic was to be a little bit crazy and unpredictable. I spent years trying to make what I thought was a classical education work in my family and I did this without any outside help or classes. We just didn't have the money for those sorts of resources.

Then I joined an email group which discussed classical education. Women from this group, and a few brave men, were the best resource of all. They became known as "the brain trust," and that is exactly the role they played in my life -- and in the lives of many others. The best thing about the group was that they welcomed disagreements and considered them healthy. Coming from the rather isolated and somewhat fearful homeschooling community, this changed the course of my life. I was encouraged to search for Truth in life and education without fear, alongside other ladies ready and willing to hold my hand as together we climbed the Hill Difficulty.

For many years I had one foot in the classical community and one foot in the Charlotte Mason community, all the while sensing that there were a great many similarities between the two. While Mason didn't directly promote what we now call Classical Education, you will find the two fit together in quite nicely as Karen Glass illustrated in her book *Consider This*.

Ambleside Online used David Hick's *Norms and Nobility* as a model for their upper levels. *Norms* is an absolute must-read for classical and Charlotte Mason educators and is the basis for my all-time favorite Ambleside level, Year 7. Taking that book to the hospital with me when Alex was born, I found that I could not understand it...yet. It would take me a couple more tries before I finally blogged my way through the whole book and fell in love with it in the process.

But then I read Stratford Caldecott's *Beauty in the Word*, and it seemed like the stars in my classical and Charlotte Mason worlds aligned. He said what someone needed to say, and he said it beautifully. What is the purpose of the trivium? Is it so our children can rattle off lists of facts? Impress us with their knowledge of the chemical elements at age nine? I have long called these pony tricks, and here Caldecott was saying the same thing. The grammar stage of the trivium, what Dorothy Sayers has been interpreted as calling the 'poll parrot' stage, was not for memorizing, but for remembering. If you want to explore that concept in depth, read Caldecott's lovely, somebody-finally-gets-it-right book, *Beauty in the Word*.

When Caldecott used the word 'remembering' in place of the word 'grammar' everything began to make sense, to come together. Morning Time was for remembering, and re-membering is the most profoundly significant thing we do in education. If we are going to have a dialectic 'stage' and a rhetoric 'stage' which don't produce monsters, then we are going to have to build it all on a platform of remembrance. Remembrance includes memorizing, but it is ever-so-much more. It is the difference between "lightening and the light-ening bug," as Samuel Clemens used to say.

If we understand the difference between memorizing and remembrance, then it will help us choose what to memorize. Remembrance is culture. It is all that has come before that makes us the kind of people we are. To not remember is to commit cultural suicide, which is what we see when we look at our culture today. I don't want want to start you into a panic with my hand-wringing, but if we don't understand our times, then we will have nothing left to do but wring our hands. When the Titanic was sinking there was no time left to build another boat. Rescue could only come by using the materials available.

Like it or not, our children are growing up in this culture. They are moving into the future away from us, just as we moved into the future away from our parents. Our children cannot live in our time. They live in their own time, but the more tied to the past they are in their mind, the safer they will be; the more wisdom they will have. You can have grammar, logic, and rhetoric without having wisdom— but why would you want to?

We have a limited time to help our children fill the backpack they will carry into the future. The chemical elements are useful, but they have little meaning to a child of ten. To teach a child to memorize what does not have meaning is, in my opinion, insane. We are trying to teach them that learning matters. Knowledge is meaningful. We do this by connecting them to what is meaningful to them. In the early years, we want to feed their minds with stories of all kinds—through history, Bible, poems, songs, imaginative fiction, family traditions. We want to tell them these stories and let them tell them back to us. A wise person once said, "Raise up a child in the way he should go and in the end, he will not depart from it." That is remembering.

One of my favorite photos is one where Alex is just home from a baseball game and still in his uniform. He is sitting on the couch holding his little sleeping niece Bella while talking to his grandfather on the phone. That picture brings me great comfort. I know that Alex will have a hard time untethering himself from the past when the evil days approach.

Last night I went to bed rather discouraged. I couldn't put my finger on exactly why, but I think it had something to do with the pervasiveness of the culture in our home. For years, we had tried to live a counter-cultural life. We failed. Sometimes we failed because we wanted our children more than we wanted our counter-culture. The whole point of the counter-culture was to preserve our children from a wicked and perverse generation.

Anyone who knows me, knows I tend to think too much. But something happened in my thinking when Andrew Kern said, "The radical pulls the child out of the culture. The conservative tries to weave the child into the culture." Anyone who knows Andrew knows he was speaking about *The Odyssey.* For the first time, I got a glimpse of why our counter-cultural lifestyle had failed and how there was maybe no such thing as a culture war. To fight against the culture is to commit suicide. We live in this culture. To pretend our children will live in another culture is insanity. But still, I worry about my children. Lately, I have seen evidence of families losing their children's hearts. I have talked to many, many moms grieving for children who have left the faith. Good moms. Good families.

And then last night, I glanced at a quote from John Senior about destroying the television. We had lived for twenty-five years without a television, and the benefits were evident, and yet I know that now that we have one we cannot get rid of it, nor do I think we should. I wish we 'should' but I know we shouldn't. Knowing I could not change our reality left me deeply depressed for my children.

Last night, I was reading and praying and in the midst of it I prayed, "My children, Lord, O, my children." Then, today, in a twinkling, God took all my reading and all my thinking and all my praying and showed me something true and something hopeful and maybe even the whole shebang.

Today, one of my children, an older one visiting for the weekend, was talking to his grandfather on the phone. That is it. I don't know how to explain this, but the second I heard that child, I felt a great peace. That child was rooted. That child may be a sloppy mess sometimes, but he is rooted. That child has a grandfather with whom he talks. And suddenly I know how to handle this cultural tide against which I cannot stand. I do not have to stand against it. I have to make sure we are rooted in real things. I can't fight Facebook, but I can plant a tomato. Every single time I do something that anchors our family to the past and our heritage, I am helping preserve the hearts of my children. I am giving them a lifeline to the good life. We don't have our children for long. We don't have a whole lot of control over their lives or their futures. When we plant our flags on issues, we often win the battle and lose the war. I have not been able to justify losing the war by taking stands on issues, even issues I care deeply about. Love and heritage are good; issues not so much. If my children are tied to our family by love, then all will be well, even if they don't always plant their flags where I have planted mine.

And this is what I have been reading about in so many places: Edith Schaeffer's *The Hidden Art of Homemaking*, Stratford Caldecott's *Beauty in the Word*, and Kevin Clark and Ravi Jain's *The Liberal Arts Tradition: A Philosophy of Christian Classical Education*. Education is tethering our children to the past so that they are not adrift in the universe. That's it. Hug your children, especially your older ones. Listen to them. Tell them stories.

Last year Alex found a wild blackberry patch behind our house. I was excited because I had picked blackberries with my grandfather. My grandmother used to make a blackberry cobbler, and it was my favorite food. When Alex brought me the blackberries, I made a cobbler and told him how I picked blackberries with my grandfather.

This year, he reminded me it was time to pick blackberries again. I did not have to nag him into it. So he picked them again and  I told him about my grandfather and my grandmother again and then I made another cobbler. That is a tether. That is an education.

You can't fight your children into the Kingdom. You can pray for them, and you can tell them stories, and you can love them.

§

I am going to try something new this year. When my children scare me with their cultural laxity or their strange ideas (you know, tattoos and stuff), instead of fighting with them, I am going to hug them and tell them a story, and, of course, keep praying for them.

We stand in the gap between our children and all that came before. We are the keepers of the culture. If our culture commits suicide, we cannot wring our hands and point the finger. We are the ones responsible. We might have to avoid puffing up our children with the chemical elements in order to tell them about the time we picked blackberries with our grandfather. There is plenty of time to learn The Periodic Table of Elements, but the time is fleeting to throw out hooks of remembrance, as many as we can, between our generation and the next.

But our children stand in the gap, too. They must have something to throw to the next generation, to their children, or our culture will die. Perhaps we even need to throw out more hooks than our parents threw to us since the keepers of culture are passing away. We may be few, but we know that the "fewer we are the greater share of glory." We are not those who shrink back at long odds. We are those who press towards the mark, knowing that while our own efforts could never 'save' our children, our faithfulness is a means of grace.

One of my favorite pieces of advice boils down to 'Just do it.' So often mothers worry about what they are not doing. I hear these things all the time:

"I don't read aloud to my children." "I can't seem to find time to have my devotions." "We never take nature walks." "Narration is too hard to add to our school day."

To these moms, I say, "get up right now and do THAT thing." Today, now, put down this book and have your child immediately write a narration or have your devotions or take a walk. Once we took a nature walk in a raging storm to quell the raging frustration in my heart at our lack of nature walks. That walk will go down in the annuls of remembrance for me, my children, and even my future son-in-law whose happy attitude pulled me to the top of that mountain when all I could do was visualize the helicopter rescue.

When it comes to all of these nagging things, we only have to do a small bit today and tomorrow and the next day to look up one day and find we have accomplished something unthinkably huge. You don't have to read the whole Bible today or this year. All you have to do is pick up your Bible right now and read a few verses.

For me, planning and chore charts and all those big plans were only mildly helpful in life, often taking more upkeep than the chore itself. As I described already, I always assigned permanent jobs to my children. I did not have time to wade through the chore chart and the arguments. If James always does the dishes, then there is no argument over who did them last. James did. End of story. End of chore chart. End of constant distraction. More time for reading aloud.

Often our planning keeps us from living. You don't have to plan a read-aloud to start one. You can pick up a book right this minute. Just shut this one and do what I do: holler, "Attention!!"

# CHAPTER ELEVEN

# All My Friends Are Dead

*"The person, be it gentleman or lady, who has not pleasure in a good novel, must be intolerably stupid."*
**Jane Austen,** *Northanger Abbey*

*I*t is now, and I suspect always will be, the greatest achievement in my life that I taught all my children to read. I loved teaching them to read. For years, I used a notebook and Alphaphonics, later adding *Teach Your Child to Read in 100 Easy Lessons*. I am not fond of that whole book, but the early lessons are perfect for a child who knows all the sounds but can't blend them together. Eventually, I settled on using some form of the Spalding Method with each child. It is a slow simmer and the most thoroughly effective. It is a broad, strong, logical foundation.

I owned many sets of little readers, and I believe that was important. Of course, *Bob Books* remained our favorites—almost like old family read-alouds, making their way into our collective conscience.

Over the years, I learned more than I ever taught. In this

way, homeschooling was a selfish pursuit for me. Our home was a strong bastion of the liberal arts, and, in that way, it was a good base for further learning, if not an end all in itself. We were feeble in the maths and sciences, although that didn't stop one of my sons from majoring in nuclear engineering. The only advice I dish out on those subjects is, "Seek outside help." But, even so, there is nothing wrong with laying down a wide and generous foundation on which your children can build their lives.

Few schools can duplicate the home when we moms and dads understand true education. When we speak idealistically about "true" education, the home cannot be beaten. But there comes a time, especially for boys, when the home is probably not enough, so it doesn't matter how ideal a learning place it is. When a boy stops learning at home, it is time to seek other options. Ideally, the other options should be found before the boy gets tired of your voice. Think of it like short lessons. Always leave them begging for more.

Most older moms I have talked to agree. Eleventh and twelfth grades are tough at home. Not because the subject matter is difficult but because of the developmental age of the boy/man. It is helpful to let him knock his head against new walls, preferably before those critical years.

As I end my homeschooling career so many things start to come into focus.

I have homeschooled for so many years by now it's hard to get a count. Do I count from when I first heard Raymond Moore on the radio thirty-four years ago? I like to think so, even though I was still a couple of years away from having children. Maybe we could count from when I started educating myself in the DeLand Public Library forty-five years ago. A more reasonable date would be from when I started Morning Time when my oldest was four, making it twenty-seven years ago. When we understand the nature of true education, we understand the numbers differently.

I suppose that I should have raked in a lot of wisdom and knowledge, and yet, the further up and further in I go the less sure I am about what I know. I know a lot less today than I did thirty-five years ago. In my weaker moments, this causes me to panic and buy Kindle books and reserve too many library books and re-read Dante and *The Faerie Queen* all in the same week, as if I had the time to catch up. After all of these years, I don't know as much as I thought I did, but I hope that makes what I do know more valuable.

Here is what I do know, what I am willing to share with you. There are three things that cover a multitude of sins: reading, reading aloud, and written narration.

Reading is the most obvious, and I will not go into it here. I hope you and your children are readers. I hope you read books, and listen to audiobooks, and recite poetry, and study history, and revel in novels. I hope you have a library card. I hope you read books for you and not just for your children. I hope you read the Bible. And if you are pregnant or nursing, I hope you won't feel guilty when you can't read. There are a few seasons in life when reading must quietly wait her turn. Don't make her wait too long, though. I loved to read while nursing my babies, at least until they started batting at the book trying to get my full attention. Babies are better than books.

When life got so busy that I didn't have time to read to

myself anymore, I began reading aloud to my children. It has been the chief joy of my life, superseded only, perhaps, by the joy I felt when my son came home talking about reading *The Princess and the Goblin* to his little girls, and I got to pull *Little House in the Big Woods* off the shelf and say, "I think they are ready for this." *The Princess and the Goblin* AND *Little House in the Big Woods*. Can there be a world with so much joy?

A few years ago, when some things in our family went awry for a while, I kept thinking, "Nothing can take away the hours we spent in those other worlds, those better countries." We will always have Narnia.

Although Charlotte Mason was not a fan of children's picture books, I am, proving I can think for myself sometimes. When Timothy was five, he started coming with me to library sales, and we amassed the best in children's literature, most of which I learned about from Gladys Hunt's *Honey for a Child's Heart*. It was my field guide to books. It didn't take Timothy long to figure out what made a good book, too. Sadly, many libraries have sold the best books to make room for Goosebumps and children's biographies of Margaret Sanger.

I read these picture books we collected over and over again until I had memorized many of them. They became the voices in my head. The characters in these books became our friends. When the grandbabies were born and their parents starting trying to find those same books for their family libraries, I was gratified.

Sometimes random books would become favorites: *Jack Jouette's Ride, The Queen Who Did Not Like to Bake Gingerbread, Lentil, Anatole, The Church Mice, Little Tim and the*

*Brave Sea Captain, Obadiah*. When I read *Obadiah* out loud during a cold winter's day, I almost always had to get up and bake a loaf of bread. The book filled me with longing for something indefinable—maybe truth, goodness, and beauty. I loved finding books of fables and fairytales and frequently haunted that part of the picture-book section at the library. Books by Margaret Hodges and Arnold Lobel, The D'Aulaires, and the Haders. *Andy and the Lion* retold the classic of *Androcles and the Lion* and was a favorite of almost everyone in my family. Who can resist grandpa saying, "And then I gave him both barrels!"?

In the same vein, the boys loved *The Biggest Bear* by Lynd Ward. It is not a magic trick that I know the words to many of these books by heart. I have memorized the books by reading them. No plan, no scheme, just reading them over and over and over again until I cannot even think, "The sun did not shine…" without running through at least ten more pages in my mind of *The Cat in the Hat.*

That is how memory and remembrance work, and that is how they were designed to operate by their Creator. We are what we behold. We memorize what we hear and read a lot. It is why we want to spend time reading the true and the good and the beautiful to our children. They have an appetite, and so do we. There is no trick to memorization. It is at the heart of all we do and say and know about education.

I love nursery rhymes. My mother and my grandmother read them to me and I read them to my children and grandchildren. They resonated with the beat of my heart. One day recently I repeated, "Jack and Jill went up the hill," and my little granddaughter already knew the rest of the verse. I happily pulled out my pony trick and taught her the mostly un-read second verse. Now she loves to sing, "vinegar and brown paper" with me. Perhaps that is just a little thing, but in many ways, it is everything I want for her.

Long before a child can read for himself, his mind is ready for headier materials than picture books afford. He is ready for longer books that cannot be read in one sitting, or two or three. He is ready for chapter books. His understanding sur-passes his abilities; this is a wonderful time because often the books that stimulate his mind also stimulate yours.

As I mentioned earlier, for twenty-five years we did not have a TV. It began as an experiment. We were moving tem-porarily to Massachusetts and putting most of our belong-ings into storage. On a whim, I said, "Let's put the TV in stor-age!" with as much enthusiasm as I could muster to trick my husband into complying. My original thought was, let's see if we get bored without one. We didn't. We read. This was no sacrifice on my part, but Tim loved football season. He gen-erously gave up something he loved for us and, in the end, we all benefitted greatly.

Earlier, I described the year that Timothy was four, when I began reading longer books to him. We read during morning time, nap times, meal times, and in the evenings before bed. Reading was the framework of our lives. I believe it developed the minds of the children in ways that are immeasurable. I of-ten joke that Timothy read too many boy-against-the-world books, and he grew up to be a man with the imagination to take on the world. When I start looking back over the titles we read, it is almost as if there are strong bonds of truth hold-ing us to one another even when time, space, and ideology separates us. I may have chased one of my sons around the house with a broom, but I also read *Smoky the Cowhorse* to him.

Deep inside I believe that reading aloud covers a multitude of sins. It is a grace. When we cannot escape ourselves, we can escape to other worlds together. My husband has many regrets about the times he, tired from working long hours, was exacting on the children, but he doesn't regret the hot summer nights sitting in the back yard reading *Treasure Island* aloud.

I may be too serious and way too philosophical; I may have over-spiritualized and preached when I should have kept quiet, but I laughed my head off at the antics of a boy named Penrod. You could say Penrod saved me from me.

When you spend years and years reading aloud, especially when your life is absent from other distractions, the places and the people in books become family friends. You talk about them like you know them.

When I was in college, my mom wrote me updates on our favorite soap opera, *Days of our Lives*. I was reading one of the letters out loud to Tim who was then my boyfriend, when he stopped me and said, "This is terrible. So many sad things are happening to your friends." I looked at him, puzzled, before laughing. My mom's letter had seamlessly moved from soaps to real life with no warning. I can imagine the historical confusion these kinds of letters would produce.

But characters often seem like our friends, don't they?

Christopher was a funny little fellow who loved to read. He was always asking questions like, "Were you alive in Jesus's time?" Our life was so literary in those days, and Christopher had been in Morning Time since he was a week old, so I guess his imagination had not worked out who was who for most events. To make matters worse, I was always saying we lived in a house where George Washington could have visited.

One day, Chris asked me if George Washington was still alive. In disbelief, I answered, "No, Christopher, he died a long time ago."

He looked at me so sincerely and said, "All my friends are dead."

Then there is the problem large families face of imagining that once you read something everyone remembers it even if they weren't born yet.

Once, six year old Emily mused, "I wonder who the first man was?"

I was appalled.

"Emily, you know who the first man was: Adam!"

She calmly replied, "Never heard of him."

I pulled out the Bible story book that day.

A few years ago I asked each family member to name their favorite read-alouds. You can find this list on my old blog archives at Morning Time Moms on Blogspot, but a few books appeared over and over again.

*Little Britches, The Wind in the Willows, The Chronicles of Narnia, Penrod, Farmer Boy.*

What reading family cannot, with consensus, separate their family members into book characters? Puddleglum and Eeyore, Toad and Pa, Uncle Andrew and Almanzo, Reepicheep and Sam Gamgee. These depictions help us recognize one another and understand one another, perhaps they even allow us to see the Eustace Scrubbs in our midst and maybe even forgive them. After all, not everyone has read the right books.

If you worry that you haven't read the right books, no matter how old your children are, you can still pick up a book and start reading. Don't keep the children too long, but do try to find the right sort of book. Maybe *The White Company* or *Robin Hood* or something by E. Nesbit. Read to them for ten minutes or so and let them go. No need to talk about it. Just read. The talking will come later and then even later the voices.

*"Little boy kneels at the foot of the bed droops on little hands, little gold head. Hush! Hush! Whisper who dares!..."*

*"Wynken, Blynken and Nod one night sailed off in a wooden shoe..."*

*"James, James, Morrison, Morrison, Weatherby, George Dupree...."*

*"The sun did not shine, it was too wet to play..."*

*"Once upon a time there were four little rabbits and their names were Flopsy, Mopsy, Cottontail, and..."*

*"Christopher Robin has wheezles and sneezles, they bundled him into his bed..."*

*"In the great green room..."*

*"Clam chowder for lunch!!!!"*

*"In all of France, there was no mouse more beloved than Anatole..."*

*"It was very early Christmas morning, and in the stillness of the dawn, with the soft snow falling on the housetops, a little child was..."*

*"Little Black you are the best pony in the whole world...."*

*"Listen my children and you shall hear of the midnight ride of Paul Revere..."*

*"I never really knew Father very well until we moved to the ranch..."*

*"For God so loved the world..."*

*"Christmas won't be Christmas without any presents..."*

*"They tell us, Sir, that we are weak, unable to cope with so formidable an adversary..."*

*"Marley was dead; dead as a doornail..."*

*"The Lord is my shepherd..."*

*"Where is he that wishes so? My cousin Westmorland?.... If we are marked to die, we are enough...."*

Those are the voices in my head, and in the heads of my children. Someday, perhaps, those words will still be there for my children and me when we have forgotten all else—the torch of culture passed and shared from one mind to another.

§

I read to the children, yes, but I also read for my own education and enjoyment. All my friends are dead, too.

When I was a young girl my mother bought a set of Companion Library books from a traveling salesman. She often mentioned it with disgust, disapointed in herself for how little resistance she had to the salesman. But I see them as providential. I read most of the books found in the set over and over again: *Little Women*, *A Dog of Flanders*, *The Wizard of Oz*, *The Five Little Peppers and How They Grew*, and others.

I spent the early years of our marriage reading George MacDonald. I consumed every book of his I could get my hands on, especially looking for volumes that had not been updated for modern language. *Phantastes* remained my favorite book throughout my twenties and always in the back of my mind is the hope that I will someday have time to return to MacDonald's works.

As family life started I read Edith Schaeffer's *Hidden Art* and *L'Abri*. I even read her volumes of letters. I read every book I could get my hands on about pregnancy and birth, and I particularly I loved Sheila Kitzinger's books. I always kept a policeman's handbook ready for any extra-quick births. I am just a tiny bit disappointed the midwife always made it on time.

Every summer I tried to read an inspiring homeschool book, my favorite of which was Laura Berquist's *Designing Your Own Classical Curriculum*. Laura writes with that perfect mix of motherly compassion and practical help.

Eventually, murder mysteries became my favorite novels. Ellis Peters' Cadfael books are great fun and well-written; P.D. James is a writer of profound talent; and, of course, there is the most astute mystery writer of all: Dorothy Sayers. I suspect that in a life as chaotic as mine was, the idea of someone *not* getting away with something was like a drug.

About fifteen or twenty years ago I read the books of Helene Hanff. *84, Charing Cross Road* details her correspondence with British Bookseller, Frank Doel, who worked for Marks & Co. Doel helped Helene buy and read great British literature. After twenty years of letters, she longed to meet him in person and to see the bookshop. So she made the trip to England in 1971 at the age of fifty-five. But, sadly, Frank Doel was dead by that time, and the bookshop closed. Still, her trip of a lifetime is chronicled in *The Duchess of Bloomsbury Street*.

While reading Hanff's books I closely identified with her story of a woman pursuing self-education, and I dreamed that, like her, I would one day have a literary vacation in England. For long years, I carried a deep yearning in my heart to see the places I had read about. Sometimes, my heart would ache with that longing and sometimes, as friend after friend traveled to England, tears would come to me in private moments. I had made other choices with my life and with my money, choices I would make again, but still, I yearned. That trip was never going to happen after all; that was ok. But God is not limited by our small worries. He creates longings, I think, and he fulfills them. Truly, we can trust him.

Recently, I filled out my passport forms and mailed them off. Then, one day, as I was pulling out of the driveway to take Alex to baseball practice, I checked the mail. I was fifty-four years old, and my passport had finally arrived for the first time. I cried all the way to practice, explaining to Alex that I was just having one of those moments. A few days before this I had received a payment for some work I had done so within hours of getting my passport, I was able to book a flight to attend a Charlotte Mason Conference in Ambleside, UK.

On Easter Sunday, 2016, I boarded a flight to London. I traveled by plane, tube, train, and taxi all by myself to the conference, where I met up with friends who would usher me through the Lake District (*Swallows and Amazons*), Oxford (The Inklings), and London (Lord Peter). I was not surprised to find my London hotel was located in Bloomsbury. I was the Duchess of Bloomsbury 2.0.

The morning I was to return home, I had not yet seen 84, Charing Cross Road. So I woke up, ate my British Breakfast (minus the baked beans), and trekked out of Russell Square by Bloomsbury Square towards Charing Cross. It took me a few minutes of searching up and down the block but I finally found the plaque dedicated to that bastion of self-education, Helene Hanff.

One of the women I was traveling with said, "You seem to know so much about the places we are visiting."

I answered, "I have been studying for this my whole life."

As I walked along the road surrounding Lake Coniston and sailed on Lake Windermere, I wasn't looking out across the lake at the Swallows and Amazon children sailing, I was looking back across the years to some other children who were sitting on the couch listening to stories. They had been here already and so had I.

CHAPTER TWELVE

# A Dillar, a Dollar

*"All virtue is a form of acting."*
**William Butler Yeats**

ince reading and reading aloud are two things homeschoolers do well, I write about them just for the fun of it. Not so widely practiced and loved is the written narration. Even mothers who follow a Charlotte Mason education struggle with practicing narration in their homes. So many times when giving mothers advice I try to get them to relax and let things go, but over the last few years I have come to such a philosophical epiphany concerning narration, especially written narration, that I urge you strongly to consider practicing it daily in your home.

There are all sorts of writing programs on the market. Teaching writing is much simpler and much harder than most of these programs understand. In fact, I believe that many of these programs hinder a genuine understanding of what writing is and what it does for a student. Writing is processing. It is thinking. *The Lost Tools of Writing* is one of the few programs that ultimately gets this. Writing is at the core of a classical education, and indeed, it is at the core of a Charlotte Mason education. Charlotte Mason did not merely suggest oral and written narration. It is the core of her philosophy. Indeed, if you skip narration you are not giving your child a Charlotte Mason education. This is not to discourage you. It is to help you prioritize your school days.   Narration is synthesis. It is taking what we read and processing it with our minds. If we read a book knowing we have to tell someone else about it, we will read with attention. Without attention, no child or adult learns anything. Narration, oral and written, trains the mind to pay attention. The attention the child gives engages his mind so that he is not merely reading, he is processing what he is reading. Narration ensures that this happens. Without narration, the child can lazily read and immediately forget.

Ultimately, it is good for a child to narrate every single thing he reads for school, either orally or in writing. Of course, we do not have time to write out every single narration. But every child should be producing at least one written narration every day from the time they can write about five sentences.

Think of it this way: The mind is a powerful tool. If you imagine something, it is real to your mind. I remember reading about an experiment where the researchers sprayed perfume during a lecture, then later they sprayed the same perfume during an examination on the lecture for some of the students. Those who had the perfume sprayed again did better on the test. The point here is that the senses begin in the brain. They are brain signals.

Narration is the single best pedagogical tool for harnessing the power of the mind. A child who reads knowing he must narrate can have all his inner senses at his disposal for memory. A child who reads great works and narrates them back naturally starts picking up style and content along the way, even if subtly.

Working on the mechanics of writing is something we can do conversationally, using a white board and short lessons. Mechanics are not processing or thinking. They are means to communication, but they are not the thing itself. You can hold a child accountable for any mechanics he has learned (i.e., always start a sentence with a capital letter), but a child who has great mechanics will never be a good writer if he has not learned to think and process, and narration is the ideal tool for ensuring that this happens. A child who has learned to process information through narration, even if he is not a naturally gifted writer, will be comfortable both thinking and writing.

You do not need to spend years and years teaching formal writing, but you should, without any exceptions, have your children narrate, both orally and in writing, every school day. Have them narrate every single day over ten years or so and your children will be comfortable thinkers and writers. It is a simple solution, but it will not work if enacted sporadically. Narrating has to be at the heart of the school day. So many things can go by the wayside, but narration is the heart of a classical education. Indeed, written narration can, if necessary, be Latin and logic in the too-stretched homeschool.

When I finally began to understand this, I started saying

that it was like a magic trick. It seemed that way to me. Then I read Charlotte Mason's own words, and she said the same thing in *Towards a Philosophy of Education*: "This, of telling again, sounds simple, but it is really a magical creative process by means of which the narrator sees what he has conceived, so definite and so impressive is the act of narrating that which has been read only once. I dwell on the single reading because let me repeat, it is impossible to fix attention on that which we have heard before and know we shall hear again."

Narration is the magic key to thinking. Give up whatever you need to teach from that elusive state of rest, but do not give up narration.

Oral narration can begin as soon as a child begins to tell stories on his own. This can be quite young for some children and not so young for others. Children are born persons, right? To do it properly, set aside some time during your read-aloud period, such as during Morning Time. After each read-aloud (and I recommend they be short) request an oral narration from one of the students, making sure they do not know ahead of time which student will be selected to narrate, and not letting the talkative ones (yes, we all have one) hog up all the time. Ask the chosen narrator to repeat back, in his or her own words, what he or she heard in the reading. There are no right or wrong answers. You are not looking for specific information as in a workbook; you are challenging and stretching their memories and their minds.

When a child is nine or ten you can begin written narration. I usually had my children write five sentences each day, in which they responded to a book we were reading. "I liked this book," is not a good narration sentence. A ten year old might write:

*In* Little Pilgrim's Progress *today, Christian and Hopeful came to the dark river. They were afraid. Hopeful held Christian's hand. They made it to the Celestial City. Little Christian saw his mother.*

Per Charlotte Mason's ideals, I would personally change any incorrect spellings without pointing them out to the child. I would explain how to spell the word after I corrected it on my own, never drawing attention to the misspelled word.

Many boys will not love this time of writing, but it is absolutely essential that it be a given, no-questions-asked, each day. It may not be pretty or even particularly well thought-out, but it must be done daily. If you want to spend the rest of your school days fighting with your child over writing, make this exercise infrequent and optional.

As the child becomes comfortable writing, you can increase the length of the written narration until eventually a high school student will be writing five to seven hundred words (or more) a day in a reading journal. Even in high school these journals should not be critiques of the book but simple retellings, although you can allow your students to give opinions here and there. You will also notice they often imitate the style of the writer they are reading as they write in these journals, which is beneficial.

If you are teaching another writing program with your high school students, I recommend you still require the daily written narration or reading journal.

Before we started written narration in our home, we did

copy work. Copy work encourages the child to recognize good writing and to imitate it. I haven't talked much about imitation, but in a classical Charlotte Mason school, the whole of language arts, poetry, spelling, and style are based on imitation.

You may wonder how things will turn out if you take this minimalist approach. I finally felt at peace with the power of narration when my son James was writing his Senior Integration Paper at Covenant College. It was about thirty-five pages long and I was not looking forward to reading it. Thirty-five pages of academic writing does not sound like a good evening. The title of the paper was called *Swung On and Belted* and was about the explosive statistics in baseball during the 1990s.

A few pages in, I was enjoying the paper and for days afterwards I was using what I had learned in it while at the ball field. I even explained the changing strike zone to a mom who was complaining about the umpire. This is what happens when introverts venture out in public. I had enjoyed reading the paper, and I found the knowledge fun and useful, but I worried that the professors at Covenant would think the paper was not academic enough because it was not dry. In truth the other academic SIP I had heard was a bit dry and full of theory. You could tell this other paper was well-organized, academic, and written by a highly intelligent person, but it was not compelling. I wondered if the fact that James's paper was all of those things would be lost because it was interesting and enjoyable.

But it turned out that my fears were needless. Both students assigned to critique his paper knew nothing about baseball but seemed to appreciate his efforts to make his paper understandable. They gave great feedback and I paid attention to what they said.

James's oral presentation went as well as possible with lots of lively questions afterwards, which he answered with ease and competence. His professor seemed to enjoy the paper, even suggesting that he turn it into a book.

While driving home I began to think about homeschooling and how much credit I could take for James's success. I am always trying to justify my existence. It occurred to me that the writing skills all of my children have displayed at one time or another were not so much the product of what we had done but rather what we had not done. We had missed some important things along the way, especially in the areas of grammar and usage, but the boys have all been able to overcome that in college. In the midst of reading thousands of good books and writing hundreds of narrations, the children had never learned to write badly. They had never developed the stilted style of the format writer. It turns out that it was not so much what we did do in our home as what we didn't do. What we don't do may be the real key to our success, I mean, the success of our children.

Thank you, Charlotte Mason.

# CHAPTER THIRTEEN

# A Long Time Ago

*"All shall be well, and all shall be well,*
*and all manner of thing shall be well."*
**Julian of Norwich**

*I* went to see a counselor a few years ago and was
annoyed that she kept insisting that I needed a
chance to be 'me' and not just 'Mama.' I didn't
relate to what she was saying. I resisted her ideas because
they seemed to encourage selfishness on my part. Later, I realized that it is selfish for a mother to place her whole life in
the hands of her children. That is a burden they cannot bear.
It is important for a mother to have a life apart from her children—for her sake and for theirs.

I first learned this lesson when my oldest son left for Navy
boot camp. My brilliant blue-eyed boy had decided to join
the Navy and I was flummoxed. This had never once entered
my mind while I was homeschooling him. I had imagined
all manner of greatness for him, and none of it began with
the military. But there he was, on a bus traveling to Chica-
go, while I drove home crying my eyes out. I cried for three

days straight. I sat in Morning Time and cried. It seemed that I had worked passionately for nineteen years on a beautiful product and, in the end, he had become something entirely different than I intended. I did not recognize him at all. How could I go on creating beautiful pottery pieces if they weren't going to turn out as I intended or hoped? But, life being what it is, I still had to get up in the morning and pretend. I kept on pretending, my passion and vision in tatters, until one day I had an epiphany. I was not the potter. A potter was shaping my children, but it was not me.

I had forgotten what Charlotte Mason wrote: "Children are born persons."

Until that moment, I had not heard her with my heart nor truly understood with my mind. My son was not my product. He was the work of a great artist: the Creator of all.

It was a glorious moment.

After I got over the insult of it, I began to feel much lighter and happier. You could almost hear me singing, "Ding Dong the witch is dead." I had misunderstood my role as a mother and as a teacher, and it would still take me a while to understand how to go about not being the potter. I was going to have to go back and re-read Charlotte Mason with fresh eyes.

When you tell your story, you like to tell the good parts, the funny parts. It is not inauthentic to leave out sad things. In the olden days, that was called airing your dirty laundry. I prefer to air our family's dirty laundry privately, but don't let that make you think there is none. That is the problem, though, isn't it? We romanticize other people's lives while depreciating our own. Homeschool mothers are good at this. We hear what another mom does for crafts or math, and we imagine that not only is she good at those things but she has all our own priorities, as well. We make up a composite ho-meschool mom in our minds. She is good at everything. She does not go to bed at night with that infernal list of didn't-dos looping through her dreams. We know this is inaccurate, but the imagination is powerful. We want to believe in perfect families.

The greatest benefit I see from our homeschooling years is the closeness of the children. Their ongoing sibling Snap-chats kind of make me jealous. I often threaten to join Snap-chat just to be a part of their camaraderie. It's funny to watch the horror on their faces when I suggest this.

§

One of my favorite illustrations of family life is in Terence Malick's film, *The Tree of Life*. In it, Brad Pitt plays a pret-ty terrible father, and his family suffers the consequences of his actions, including bitterness. The Bible says to beware the root of bitterness because it is deadly. Not much worthy of redemption was in that family once bitterness took hold. But in spite of that, the movie concludes with the perfect picture of redemption. After all the pain and suffering, all the anger and bitterness, the members of the family, one by one, join each other on a bright beach. All of the family members are there, the good and the bad. They greet each other joyful-ly because now they truly are what eluded them before: the perfect family.

Right now, here on Earth, we play Happy Families, and that is okay, because we are rehearsing. Someday our families, yours and mine, will be perfect when we reunite with our true Father, face to face.

Most mothers like to think there are perfect families out there. It makes them hopeful, but what *should* make them hopeful is that there are no perfect families yet. There is only redemption, offered to you and your family through Jesus Christ.

Today I am taking an unexpected to trip to see my dad. His health is failing. His time is running out. Mine is too, and so is yours. After Christopher was born, I was feeling tired and emotional. Our child seemed so vulnerable. I said to Tim, "I am afraid he is going to die," and he wisely said to me, "He is." It was a strangely encouraging comment.

In many ways, we live among the ruins. Because of that, it is often difficult to see what it is we are supposed to be doing. Years ago, a Christian leader accused the homeschool movement of promoting the family as an idol. In some ways that was a fair accusation, especially when each family makes up its own religious unit based on authority rather than servanthood. That sort of thinking about the family is idolatrous and disastrous to its members. But it does not follow that because we can idolize the family, the family is not essential to Christianity. Anyone who has heard me speak knows that I believe that ideas have consequences, but isn't it also true that consequences lead to ideas?

The Mars Hill Audio Journal ran an interview in volume 119 with Mary Eberstadt concerning her book *How the West Really Lost God: A New Theory of Secularization,* which makes the case that the decline of the family is a precursor to the decline of Christianity, not always the other way around.

When the family loses meaning in society, Christianity loses meaning for the people who make up families. She said in the interview:

> It is commonplace to observe that ideas have conse-
> quences, that theories often lead to practices, that what
> we think about something will shape how we behave. It
> is not as well recognized that ideas have antecedents,
> that practices often lead to theories, that the way we are
> used to behaving will establish intuitions that guide our
> thinking. Ideas explicitly expressed in the form of state-
> ments or arguments are often the way we articulate a
> set of instinctual pre-verbal assumptions about reality.
> Assumptions that have been acquired by the experience
> of the patterns of everyday life.

"Ideas influence behavior and patterns of behavior influence ideas."

"Family decline powers loss of faith."

We are seeing the beginnings of the non-family. In secularized countries like Sweden we are seeing more and more single-person households. It is not a country of thriving families but rather a series of individuals. And, meanwhile, Japan is looking more and more androgynous. The roles of male and female are becoming fuzzy.

"Changes in family formation are driving religious belief."

§

Several years ago, during Thanksgiving at my sister Jody's house, I conversed with a group of Chinese teachers visiting America. These non-Christian women were fascinated by our large family and by homeschooling. They asked question after question, and finally one of them said to me, "I worry about my son because not only does he not have siblings but in one generation we have lost all concept of cousins or aunts and uncles." I had never thought about how quickly a society changes with a one-child policy. In one generation whole swaths of family life are removed. We are living in a rapidly crumbling infrastructure.

This also brings us around to the idea put forth by George Gilder in *Men and Marriage,* that the most destructive force in the world is the single male. Children make us better people and often better Christians. This is all part of that tether I keep talking about. Our children are tethers, too. They hold us to the past, to our heritage, to our Christianity. As strange as it sounds to our modern ears, we are saved through childbearing (I Timothy 2:11). Motherhood is a high calling. Civilization depends upon motherhood. I do not believe you should lose yourself so thoroughly in your motherhood that that is all you are. That is not healthy for you or your family. But I do think women need to know that motherhood is a high-value commodity in the market of civilization.

Mama, you are the first pillar of education. You are a vital part of the infrastructure of culture, family, and even the body of Christ.

This is not about having the perfect family or the perfect school. Your success or failure doesn't rest on your perfection, just your faithfulness. Your family is going to be a mess sometimes. You could cure this, of course, by not having a family at all, which is the modern choice. Western Civilization does not rest on perfect families but on imperfect ones. Your family and mine.

When I look at my children and their children, I feel proud, but not of myself or my husband or our family. I am proud of my children as individuals who stand alone before their Creator just as I do. A wise person once said not to take too much credit or too much blame for your children. That is comforting. This is often hard for the homeschooling mom, because she has laid down her life. Her reputation and even her abilities are on the line. It is an incredible burden to carry. Traditional school sometimes looks like the place where everything is not her fault.

In all of the world, there is nothing quite like motherhood. A mother has a baby and ever-after her heart clings to that child. I believe God understands the heart of a mother. He does not rebuke Rachel when she weeps for her children.

Part of the sanctification of motherhood is learning to trust God with our children. One day we will come to the end of what we can do for our children. In those early days our children cannot live without us, but slowly they grow up and move away. This is almost always heart-wrenching, but the process also gives us a chance to lean on our Heavenly Father and to trust Him more. God has entrusted us with a great treasure. It is our life lesson to hand it back. To let it go. Our children must not become 'Our Precious.' In the end, we are merely mothers. Mothers who are also children of our Father. Let us run into His arms with great joy, knowing that when we see Him face to face, we will not be standing alone.

§

One of the most hauntingly beautiful passages in all of American literature comes at the end of *Little House in the Big Woods*. Laura had been listening to her parents speak of old times, and now Pa is playing the fiddle. As Laura drifts off to sleep, she thinks, "…this is now. It can never be a long time ago."

A long time ago now, about last Friday, Laura was a little girl. When my daughter was born, my grandmother was eighty-four. She loved riding in the rumble seat; my daughter loves surfing the Internet. Now, suddenly, my intense mothering years are almost over. I am a grandmother of ten already.

The great secret older women keep is that adult children can cause more anxiety than toddlers; the good news is you get more sleep. The role of the older mother is prayer. My mother-in-law often told me she was praying for me. When she died it felt like a giant vacuum was left in the universe. With ten grandchildren, living across the length and breadth of the United States, I cannot always afford to be what I imagine as the perfect grandmother, but that doesn't diminish my love. My immediate family Christmas gift list numbers twenty-one. How can I, with presents and gifts, show twenty-one people that I love them deeply? It is impossible. My heart lavishly loves, but my paltry gifts cannot bear the burden of that love. The greatest gift I can give is prayer. When I am tempted to fear for my large family, I take my anxieties and by prayer and supplication with thanksgiving, I let my requests be made known to God, and the peace of God, which truly surpasses all understanding guards my heart and my mind in Christ Jesus.

But that is not all. No, that is not all.

Homeschooling has grown and morphed since those early days. Moms don't have to take on the whole brunt of it anymore. There are co-ops which meet one, two, three, or four days a week. Even traditional schools are noticing that the Internet has changed where and when children learn. There is still the danger of substituting busyness for true learning, but that is something we will always have to navigate in these utilitarian days. It is still all about getting your philosophy right.

Remember the old saying about the teacher learning more than the student? On my recent trip to England I traveled with several semi-retired homeschooling moms. What a "motherlode" of wisdom and knowledge they held. Each of us could fill in the gaps of the others as we observed everything from statues to wildflowers. It was astounding, the knowledge these women have accumulated over the years.

Josef Pieper tells us that leisure is the basis of culture. Most moms would laugh at the idea of leisure, but that is essentially the gift homeschooling gave us—the leisure to learn. Homeschooling moms are what remains of the leisured classes in these hurried, frantic days. We are the Irish monks of our time, carefully preserving old library books (and even reading them). In that way it is silly for us to measure our success by the immediate results—our son's SAT scores or whether our daughter got into Harvard. While we were busy thinking of our small families, we just might have been preserving something much larger.

As I came to the end of my homeschooling career many people asked me what would I do next. How would I fill the new hours opening up before me? I didn't know. Was my life purpose over? When I had cancer, I prayed that I would live until Alex graduated from high school. I told Tim that after Alex graduated, he could just dig a hole in the backyard and bury me. My limited imagination could not see the future after my children were gone.

Suddenly, though, as doors behind me close, new doors magically appear before me. New doors and new visions. After selling most of my homeschooling materials I believed that my days of teaching were over. Then I was contacted by a head hunter looking for Charlotte Mason teachers in the Chattanooga area. My first thought was, "This guy can't be for real" and, at first, I told him I wasn't interested. But it was a legitimate opportunity, and now I head out four days a week to homeschool a delightful boy named Drake. I could not have found this job on my own if I had searched for it diligently, but even after I turned down the job, Providence kept the door open for me. I have a dream job teaching a wonderfully bright and interested boy using Charlotte Mason's timeless principles.

When I think of our family's beach, like the one at the end of Malick's *Tree of Life*, I visualize more than just my family. What if other young people were standing there with us? I have almost finished raising my children; can I rescue children orphaned in our inner cities, many of whom are growing up without hope? These children are born persons, and persons must have hope. How can I stand by while these children's futures are in peril? When their mothers are praying for a future and a hope for their children? We are at a crossroads in our country. Our cities are burning with children inside.

I want to be like the little girl Charlotte Mason told about who stood on a beach among a million starfish washed ashore by a storm throwing them back into the sea one by one. When someone told her she couldn't save them all, she answered, "No, but I can save this one."

Many, many homeschool moms are graduating from their homeschooling years. On that day when I heard Raymond Moore on Focus on the Family, many of you were listening, too. You also were on a quest to learn. Perhaps instead of resting on whatever laurels we have earned, we could run towards the roar of the most defeated parts of our communities and together find ways to instill hope into the lives of the hopeless. We may not be able to do big things, but we can do small things.

Will you run towards the roar with me?

I firmly believe that as we run, new ways will open before us and streams will once again flow in the desert. We have finished one job, but maybe there is another one ahead of us. It is not our time to rest just yet. There are new jobs and new opportunities awaiting this army of mothers who have invested their lives in the true education of their children and themselves. The possibilities are endless, because our God is infinite. We just need a mustard seed of faith in Him.

Maybe we were trained for such a time as this.

# BIBLIOGRAPHY
## *The Books That Shaped My Life*

Milne, A. A., and Ernest H. Shepard. *Now We Are Six.*

Alcott, Louisa May. *Little Women.*

Mitchell, Margaret. *Gone with the Wind.*

Schaeffer, Francis A. *How Should We Then Live?: The Rise and Decline of Western Thought and Culture.*

Hunt, Gladys M. *Honey for a Child's Heart: The Imaginative Use of Books in Family Life.*

Macaulay, Susan Schaeffer. *For the Children's Sake: Foundations of Education for Home and School.*

MacDonald, George, and Ernest H. Shepard. *At the Back of the North Wind.*

MacDonald, George. *Phantastes: A Faerie Romance.*

Lewis, C. S., and Pauline Baynes. *The Chronicles of Narnia.*

Tolkien, J. R. R., Pauline Baynes, Christina Scull, and Wayne G. Hammond. *Farmer Giles of Ham: The Rise and Wonderful Adventures of Farmer Giles, Lord of Tame, Count of Worminghall, and King of the Little Kingdom.*

Mason, Charlotte M. *Towards a Philosophy of Education.*

Schaeffer, Edith. *The Hidden Art of Homemaking.*

Schaeffer, Edith. *L'Abri.*

Cook, Roy. *101 Famous Poems: With a Prose Supplement.*

Rodabaugh, Delmer, and Agnes L. McCarthy. *Prose and Poetry of England.*

Hicks, David V. *Norms & Nobility: A Treatise on Education.*

Guroian, Vigen. *Tending the Heart of Virtue: How Classic Stories Awaken a Child's Moral Imagination.*

Caldecott, Stratford. *Beauty in the Word: Rethinking the Foundations of Education.*

Berry, Wendell, and Norman Wirzba. *The Art of the Commonplace: Agrarian Essays of Wendell Berry.*

Sayers, Dorothy L. *The Mind of the Maker.*

Sayers, Dorothy L. *The New Sayers Omnibus, Containing: The Five Red Herrings, Have His Carcase, Murder Must Advertise.*

Mayne, Michael. *Learning to Dance.*

Glass, Karen, and David V. Hicks. *Consider This: Charlotte Mason and the Classical Tradition.*

Keller, Timothy, and Kathy Keller. *The Meaning of Marriage: Facing the Complexities of Commitment with the Wisdom of God.*

Cloud, Henry, and John Sims Townsend. *Boundaries in Marriage.*

Homer, and Richmond Lattimore. *The Iliad.*

Rohr, Richard. *Falling Upward: A Spirituality for the Two Halves of Life.*

# ACKNOWLEDGMENTS

Here is the part where I apologize to my family still at home for neglecting them for six months. Thank you, Andrew, Alex, and Max. Go Sonic! Here is the part where I apologize to the rest of my children for telling this tale. We all know the reality show would be off the chain.

Thank you to each of the brave souls who married my children. We hit pay dirt with Natalia, Hannah, Vanessa, and Anibal.

I owe a debt of gratitude to many, many people who shaped my thinking over the years, probably the most influential of which is Dr. George Grant, who was my mentor long before he became my pastor when I heard his tape, *The Theology of Wonder*. For years I used, and highly recommend, his Kings Meadow Humanities for high school. He is not just a thinker, though; he practices what he preaches. He and his wife,

Karen, a hospitality writer, are a rare combination of faith in action.

I would like to thank the CiRCE Institute, both Andrew and Karen Kern, for helping me transition from introverted (backward?) thinker to trembling speaker to blossoming author. They offered the resources of CiRCE to me when they had little of their own rather than during a time of abundance and have continued to bless me over and over again. My prayers are always that God would give you back exponentially for all the trouble you have suffered with me.

Thank you to James Daniels who helped me begin to understand my boys a little better and in the nick of time.

Over the years, I have had the privilege of learning from the world's most intelligent women in an email group called Class-Ed. Truly they are a brain trust. I fear that if I mention any of them I will leave out someone amazing, but I especially want to thank Chris Finnegan for being my spiritual counselor, Kim Barnes, who was the only person I had the nerve to let read the rough draft of this book, and Beth Harvey of The Harvey Center for her generous spirit. Each member of Class-Ed seems like my best friend, and I owe all Y'all a huge debt as you well know.

Thank you to the Charlotte Mason community, most especially the Ambleside Online Advisory board which includes my good friends Wendi Capehart, Lynn Bruce, Karen Glass, Anne White, Donna-Jean Breckenridge, and Leslie Laurio. I salute you.

A huge thank you to Linda Murphy for continuing to be my friend after all these years and to God for allowing us to live close enough to 'do lunch' every once in a while.

Thank you to my lovely friend Renee Mathis for letting me room with her even when I couldn't pay and for picking out all the restaurants. Every introvert needs an extroverted friend. Renee, the hostess of learning, is mine.

A big thank you to all the sweet young moms, and some growing older (Brandy Vencel and Mystie Winckler), who encourage me to keep talking, especially the awesome young moms of our local Charlotte Mason group who faithfully prayed for me during the writing of this book.

Thank you to Ted and Kelly Alling (Drake, Mallory, and Grant) for allowing me to do what I love for a few more years and to Jeannette Tulis who stretches me to do it better.

Thanks to David Kern, my editor, bless his heart, for finally realizing I am not Hemingway and letting me be me, and to his sweet wife, Bethany, for putting up with the inordinate amount of editing (time) this book needed. David now knows far more about aging women than he ever bargained for. Somebody give this guy a raise.

Thanks to Graeme Pitman for his "sick" skills. Could his kids really be that cute?

Love and thanks to my parents, Jim and Judy Ward. My dad is quite simply one of the greatest baseball coaches of his age and a wonderful mentor. Ask anyone. My mother is a dancer and a writer and her faithfulness in practicing and improving her crafts over long years is an inspiration to me.

Thanks to my sister Jody for being my safe place and my brother Scott for his tender heart.

Thanks to all the authors of all the books that have shaped me as a person, especially C.S. Lewis and Dorothy Sayers. In my fantasies I am an Inkling married to Lord Peter.

To my husband, Tim, who shares all the credit and at least some of the blame for this family and this book. Leisure is the basis of culture, and that is the gift you gave me with your own blood, sweat, and tears. I love you even if you don't have a British accent.

# ABOUT THE AUTHOR

For almost thirty years, Cindy Rollins taught her children at home, graduating eight of her nine children from their homeschool. During these years she blogged at dominionfamily.com and ordo-amoris.com where she became known for her practice of Morning Time. Today, she writes for various publications and frequently contributes to the CiRCE Institute, speaking at their conferences. She also can be found on The Mason Jar podcast with David Kern, where they discuss all things Charlotte Mason. Cindy lives with her husband Tim, youngest son Alex, and dog Max in Chattanooga, Tennessee, where she tutors, consults on inner-city school projects, and takes her grandchildren on nature hikes. She is the 2016 recipient of the Russell Kirk Paideia Prize.

# ABOUT THE CiRCE INSTITUTE

The CiRCE Institute is a non-profit 501(C)3 organization that exists to promote and support classical education in the school and in the home. We seek to identify the ancient principles of learning, to communicate them enthusiastically, and to apply them vigorously in today's educational settings through curriculum development, a publishing imprint, teacher training, events, an online academy, a content-laden website, and more.

**Learn more:**
Website - www.circeinstitute.org
Facebook - @circeinstitute
Twitter - @circeins
Instagram - @circeinstitute